Building for
Effective Mission

Other books for effective churches by Kennon L. Callahan

Twelve Keys to an Effective Church
Outlines the twelve central characteristics of effective, healthy
churches

Twelve Keys to an Effective Church: The Planning Workbook
The best way to lead a congregation in developing an effective
long-range plan

Twelve Keys to an Effective Church: The Leader's Guide
How to lead six long-range planning sessions for your church

Twelve Keys to an Effective Church: The Study Guide
New and useful ways to work through the twelve keys

Effective Church Leadership: Building on the Twelve Keys
A new vision of leadership to revitalize the local church

*Giving and Stewardship in an Effective Church: A Guide for Every
Member*
A practical plan for putting a church on solid financial footing

Effective Church Finances
A complete guide to budgeting, fund-raising, and setting and
achieving financial goals

*Visiting in an Age of Mission: A Handbook for Person-to-Person
Ministry*
Explores fourteen different forms of visiting and helps hone
visitation skills

Dynamic Worship: Mission, Grace, Praise, and Power
Outlines the major components of effective and meaningful
worship experience

Kennon L. Callahan

Building for Effective Mission

A Complete Guide
for Congregations on
Bricks and Mortar Issues

Jossey-Bass Publishers • San Francisco

To Eugene A. McCoy, whose wit and wisdom, laughter and good spirit, joy of life, common sense, and deep love have blessed us greatly. —*Kennon L. and Julie McCoy Callahan*

FIRST JOSSEY-BASS EDITION PUBLISHED IN 1997. THIS BOOK WAS ORIGINALLY PUBLISHED BY HARPERSANFRANCISCO.

Substantial discounts on bulk quantities of Jossey-Bass books are available to corporations, professional associations, and other organizations. For details and discount information, contact the special sales department at Jossey-Bass Inc., Publishers (415) 433–1740; Fax (800) 605–2665.

For sales outside the United States, please contact your local Simon & Schuster International Office.

Jossey-Bass Web address: http://www.josseybass.com

TCF Manufactured in the United States of America on Lyons Falls Turin Book. This paper is acid-free and 100 percent totally chlorine-free.

Library of Congress Cataloging-in-Publication Data

Callahan, Kennon L.
    Building for effective mission : a complete guide for congregations on bricks and mortar issues / Kennon L. Callahan.
        p.   cm.
    Originally published: 1st ed. San Francisco, CA : HarperSanFrancisco, ©1995.
        Includes index.
        ISBN 0–7879–3872–6 (alk. paper)
        1. Church. 2.   Church buildings.   3. Mission of the church.
    4. Church facilities — Planning.   I. Title.
[BV600.2.C325   1997]
254'.7—dc21
                                                                    97-24749

HB Printing   10 9 8 7 6 5 4 3 2 1

Contents

93726

Acknowledgments

This book is for every congregation that wants to advance its mission, improve its space, and/or add new facilities. You will benefit in many ways from the suggestions presented here. Your congregation will be stronger, healthier, and more helpful in the lives of people.

I want first to acknowledge the contribution made to this book by my wife, Julie McCoy Callahan. We met in high school and share a remarkable relationship as good friends, partners, and colleagues in ministry. Her wisdom and spirit, depth and insight, and love and joy are extraordinary. This is the eleventh work we have developed together. Her contributions have been vital to each book, and she has been especially helpful with this one.

I also want to thank John Shopp, senior editor at Harper San Francisco. His sense of clarity, his editorial suggestions, and his sustained wisdom about the Twelve Keys books have contributed immeasurably.

I owe a great deal to the congregations, mission leaders, building committees, pastors, staffs, mission teams, architects, interior designers, landscapers, and contractors with whom I have worked across the years. They have contributed much to my understanding of mission and mortar.

In response to many requests, I have included specific prayers and responses at the end of each chapter. May they, and indeed may the entire book, help your congregation in its mission. The grace, peace, and hope of God be with you.

1:

The Gift of Mission

And God said, "Behold, I make all things new."
Rev. 21:5

THE GIFT

God gives us the wonderful gift of mission. Amid the anxieties and frenzies of this life, God comes to us and gives us this gift. As we search for meaning beyond the glitter and glitz and the flimsies of life, God, with amazing compassion and infinite wisdom, gives us this marvelous purpose—to serve, to reach out, to share life with others and help them fulfill their destiny in God.

In the quiet moments of life we sense this gift. In the celebratory events of life we see it. In the dark, tragic moments of life we discover it. Always, the gift is near.

We are fearful then calm. We are anxious then at peace. Sometimes our emotions are all jumbled together, and we're not sure what we're feeling. In the midst of all this, God—gracious and loving—gives us the gift of mission.

In the incarnation we behold it. Christ is born into our midst to confirm the gift. And as Christ is reborn in our hearts, we can awaken to the time of mission we live in.

In the cross, we experience the gift. The sacrifice of Christ assures us that the gift is the mission. We are not invited to triumph and glory as the world understands those things. We are not invited to so-called success and to busyness as conventional society values those things. We are invited to sacrificial mission.

In the resurrection, we claim the gift. Death has not triumphed. We can confess that we have feared death too much. We can confess that we have loved the things of this world too much. All civilizations rise and fall. The things of this world come and go. The mission of God is eternal.

LIVING IN AN AGE OF MISSION

Welcome to one of the greatest ages of mission the Christian movement has ever seen. Welcome to the first century. Welcome to the twenty-first century. Welcome to a mission time.

Christ was born into an age of mission, a bleak time of empires and soldiers, palaces and kings, a time of the lame and the deaf, the blind and the poor.

This book will help you to see all you do in mission in a new light. It will help you put your priorities into better order. It will help you maximize the effectiveness of your resources for this mission time. And it will guide you through the many decisions and choices about your space and facilities as you keep the perspective of your mission foremost.

This is the time of mission congregations, when groups of Christians acknowledge and celebrate their opportunities in a rich, full mission field. A distinguishing quality of mission congregations is the questions they ask: Who are we serving in the name of Christ? Will this be helpful in people's lives as gospel, as good news?

Mission congregations draw on the wisdom, compassion, encouragement, hope, and resources that help the mission grow. They make sure that their focus stays on those whom they serve, on those whose lives and destinies they can encourage in the name of Christ.

THE LATELY DEPARTED CHURCHED CULTURE

This is no longer a churched culture. I encourage you not to mourn its passing. Do not long for a return to those days when going to church was the thing to do. The church is never at its best in a churched culture.

The church is at home in an age of mission. That is where the church began, where its roots are. That is where the church's integrity is. That is where the church best discovers its purpose.

When churchgoing was a staple of social conformity, the church was nonetheless ill at ease and out of place. Despite all the cultural status conferred on it, the church was restless and uncomfortable in a churched culture. Yes, it has enjoyed its prominence as a cultural institution and the pedestal on which it was perched. Yet the church has realized, albeit dimly, that it is not called to be admired by the world. Intuitively it has been restless to serve, not to be served.

Whenever the church accepts the perks and the prestige, it becomes a slave of the world. It is no longer a servant in the world. It becomes beholden to the world. The danger is that it will be distracted from its mission and become a pleasant irrelevancy in the culture. Its voice becomes muted, its message muffled. The good news of joy, wonder, grace, and hope is stifled.

When the church allows itself to become a pleasant irrelevancy, it becomes simply an amiable activity for those few who may have an occasional interest. The culture can then simply ignore the church.

Fortunately God invites the church to mission direction, not worldly distractions. And, fortunately, the church retains a latent memory of how to share the mission. The church that endures beyond a churched culture is a church that knows best how to live in an age of mission. With God's help, the church rediscovers its beginnings and thus lives out its true identity as servant in the world.

There are four decisive objectives in this age of mission:

- To serve
- To claim and use our strengths
- To desire justice and peace in the world
- To rely on God's grace

The Invitation to Serve

We share the mission for the sake of the mission. We share mission in order to serve. We're not in mission as a subterfuge to get more members. The mission is done for the sake of its own integrity.

God invites us to serve, not preserve. Sometimes we allow ourselves to be distracted by issues of institutional survival. We may find ourselves drawn to this procedure or that technique as a way to stave off institutional decline. Yet we have not been called to a theology of survival; we are invited to a theology of service.

Through the incarnation, life and teachings, death, and resurrection of our Lord, we discover that the way of God is to serve. We are invited to live, not as the world lives, but in the way in which Jesus has shown us to live.

The church serves and therefore lives. When the church tries to preserve itself, just the opposite occurs. Any effort to "survive" contains the seeds of institutional death. It doesn't work to try to survive first and then try to serve. God is not inviting us to grow a little bigger before we get around to serving. The church only lives as it gives itself—in service.

BUILDING ON YOUR STRENGTHS

God invites us to claim the strengths we are blessed with. Because they are God's generous gifts to us, these strengths are sufficient unto the mission God has for us. God does not call us to mission and then leave us to our own devices, frailties, and gimmicks.

Claim your strengths. Build on them. Do better what you do best. When you build on your strengths, you build a healthy mission and a healthy congregation.

Focus on strengths rather than size. There is more to life, more to mission, than simply getting bigger, so be less absorbed with size. Some romanticize bigness. Others romanticize smallness. There is no merit in size. The merit is in sharing a mission that matches your current strengths and competencies, the gifts God has given you. When congregations focus on growing their strengths, size becomes secondary. Build on your strengths and add new ones to serve the mission. You'll find power and renewal by keeping this focus.

We are called to mission service, not simply to social service. This means that we invite people to become part of the Christian movement, to become Christian. We don't push those we serve in mission in an obnoxious, belligerent way. Nor do we pretend not to be Christians. We share our service gently and positively in the name of Christ. When we do this, by example and invitation, we claim one of the strengths with which God has blessed us.

As we reach out to people with the confidence that we have something helpful to offer, we discover more fully the mission to which God is inviting us. With compelling compassion we help with specific human hurts and hopes and thereby affect the lives and destinies of many. This is, finally, the enduring legacy of any congregation.

JUSTICE AND PEACE

God invites us to discover ways of advancing justice and peace in the world. There is much in our time in need of forgiveness, reconciliation, wholeness, and caring. Issues and concerns abound. Systems and structures, persons and movements wrestle with the tough, terrifying problems of the times.

We are invited to help with these concerns. We are not asked to focus on church growth, ignoring the lame, blind, deaf, and poor. It is not that we are called to grow bigger churches; then, having done that, to turn our attention to matters of justice and peace. By the time we have grown those bigger churches we will have forgotten the invitation.

Mission congregations are willing to put their whole future on the line for a substantive cause of justice and peace. They do so both reluctantly and gladly. Survival congregations are too preoccupied with their own survival and growth to even see the concern for justice, which God has virtually planted on their doorstep. They hurry past "the man in the ditch," intent on being busy about their own growth and decline. Mission congregations know that growing the mission is central to who we are as Christians.

GOD'S GRACE

Mission congregations have a deep understanding of the magnitude of God's grace. Mission congregations rely more on the grace of God than on the gimmicks of this world.

With the full discovery of God's grace, we are freed to exercise our best creativity and flexibility. We become more sensitive to justice and equity in the world. Trusting in the grace of God to lead us forward in the mission, we understand that the things of this world have their relative and proper place.

Mission congregations have a sense of wonder and joy over the grace of God. They seek to share the grace and the joy through sharing the mission.

Our invitation is to grow the mission, to help effectively with specific human hurts and hopes in the name of Christ. We don't do the mission to grow churches. The purpose of mission growth is to grow the mission.

When I was a child, I counted on a churched culture to deliver people to the churches. When I became an adolescent, I became preoccupied with church survival. When I became an adult, I put away childish things and discovered God's invitation to mission growth.

Know this: God has given us one of the greatest ages for mission the Christian movement has ever seen. Claim it. Your life will count in God's mission.

A PRAYER FOR MISSION

God of all that is here
           and all that is beyond,
      stir our passion,
                 deepen our compassion.
May your grace be to us
                 a drenching rain of new life.
May your hope be with us
                 like the rising sun.
May we sense the living, moving,
                 stirring presence of your spirit
                           with us now.
Call us to mission.
                 Help us to answer your call.
                      In Jesus' name, amen.

2:

Discovering Your Mission

> Now there are varieties of gifts, but the same
> Spirit; and there are varieties of service, but the
> same Lord; and there are varieties of working,
> but it is the same God who inspires them all in
> every case. *1 Cor. 12:4–6*

A MISSION ACTION PLAN

God gives us extraordinary possibilities for mission. The art
is to discover, prayerfully and compassionately, the specific
gifts for the mission to which God is inviting you.

Mission congregations develop a focused plan for mission. This mission action plan

- includes at least one specific mission focus
- builds on the congregation's gifts, strengths, compassion, and hope
- maximizes the effectiveness of the specific mission resources to be shared
- lives itself out through all areas of the congregation's witness

Congregations that are doing mission well focus their resources. They share their best mission efforts in specific ways.

Some people try to do too much too soon and quickly burn out. They've set themselves up to fail. As a result, they don't get near any kind of mission again for a long time.

It is counterproductive to try to help everybody with everything. The efforts are dispersed in too many directions. Without a focus, churches deliver only a mediocre mission.

Yes, we will be gracious and hospitable to everyone. Indeed, we will in modest ways help as many people as we can. Still, we will be wise enough to focus our best strengths and talents in the mission with which God has blessed us.

A CONGREGATION'S SPECIFIC GIFTS

God gives us the gift of mission. And it doesn't stop there. God gives us these sacred and important gifts:

- the gift to help with a specific human hurt and hope
- the gift to serve people in a certain life stage
- the gift to serve people in a relational or vocational grouping
- the gift to help with a specific societal concern

Many congregations have been blessed with one of these gifts, some with a combination. Congregations who do mission well understand that there is a variety of gifts, and they put them to use in service.

Our longings lead us to our gifts. You may sense God leading you to discover and use yours. One congregation discovered its longings and competencies—its gift—to be in mission with the specific human hurt and hope of those who wrestle with alcohol. They found out that many families with children in elementary school were struggling with this problem, and this in turn led them to a mission with this life-stage group. This then led them to the societal concern of after-school education. Sometimes God touches our lives in one place because that is where our longings are, where our best gift is. Then God leads us to a fuller mission, and as we share in mission, we find that God gives the strengths and skills for the mission as God leads us. As we share the gifts for mission with which God has blessed us, God increases our abundance of them.

Through prayer, compassion, and Bible study, you can discover the specific gifts for the mission to which God is inviting you.

A Specific Human Hurt and Hope

I use the phrase "a human hurt and hope" because wherever you find a hurt, you find a hope. And wherever you find a hope, there is usually a hurt.

Here are some examples of specific human hurts and hopes that may become your primary mission focus, your best gift for mission:

- displaced children
- family development
- latchkey children
- alcohol and drug recovery
- terminal illness
- bereavement and grief
- divorce recovery

As you prayerfully search for your gifts, you will want to consider other possibilities as well. Be specific as you think of these.

In one congregation, a woman had been a beauty operator. She felt led to share her skills in mission with persons who were in convalescent homes and unable (physically or financially) to go for barber or beauty care. She empathized with this simple human hurt and looked for volunteers to assist her. They gave their services one day a week in a nearby convalescent and retirement center. Shampoos, haircuts, manicures, pedicures—shared with compassion.

Did their church gain new members from this mission? No. Did those volunteers use their gifts selflessly and with compassion? Yes. Did their mission count as concrete, effective help with a human hurt and hope? Definitely.

Mission does not have to be a lofty enterprise. Even Jesus taught his disciples through washing their feet.

A Life Stage

Perhaps the gift God has given you is helping people in a particular life stage. This may be

- early marrieds
- families with preschoolers
- families with early elementary-age children
- families with late elementary-age children
- junior high schoolers
- senior high schoolers
- college students
- singles
- workers and professionals
- people at midlife
- those with "open horizons"
- pre-retirement people

- early retirement people
- middle retirement people
- those in late retirement
- senior adults

When we use the term *families,* we are including single-parent, double-parent, blended, separated, and divorced family groupings. Also, I use the term *open horizons* rather than *empty nest* for that stage of life. In talking with people whose children are grown and gone, I find some grieving over their going and much conversation about all the things the parents are now able to do that they couldn't before. It is more a time of open horizons. In fact their biggest fear is that their kids will move back! Sometimes they do.

You'll notice too that I list several distinct retirement stages. People between 65 and 105 move through nearly as many life stages as they did from ages 1 to 30 or 20 to 50. It's not accurate to lump everyone above 65 into one life stage.

To be sure, we seek to support people in all of these life stages. At the same time, your congregation can concentrate some of your best leadership and resources on your mission when you focus on two to four of these stages.

In your prayers, seek out the specific life stages God is inviting you or your congregation to serve in the coming years.

A Relational or Vocational Grouping

The extended family clans of an earlier time have for the most part been replaced by relational networks or "vocational villages." People gather around themselves an informal, relational network of acquaintances, friends, and "family." They create a relational network which serves to give them a sense of roots, place, belonging, family, and community. Frequently these relational and vocational networks overlap. Vocational groupings encompass many possibilities in a variety of sectors, such as

- education
- service
- business
- construction
- medicine
- sales
- law
- manufacturing
- recreation

You can share mission with an entire vocational grouping. Consider which one or two could be your primary focus, for which you have some gift, as you look to the future.

Many congregations I've known have reached into the education "vocational village" of the community. These congregations include many teachers and their families, as well as retired teachers. Some congregations share a mission with people who work in construction and have discovered their gifts for helping those who build houses and pave roads.

One congregation decided to share resources and help with a nearby teaching hospital. They developed a successful mission with the doctors, nurses, and technicians of the surgical unit in particular. You will discover many more examples.

A Societal Concern

Perhaps a specific societal concern is the mission that you sense God is inviting you to and that you have gifts for. This societal concern may be a mission priority, as a concrete outreach objective for your congregation. The issues that you feel compelled to address may be related to

- education
- the community
- justice, equity, and fairness
- families
- poverty and hunger
- illiteracy
- homelessness

You will think of others. Which one or two specific societal concerns will be your primary mission focus as you look to the future?

THE GROWING OF A LEGEND

Through the mission work of a few people in the congregation, the whole church becomes a legend on the community grapevine. This is a happy by-product of doing mission effectively. The making of a legend doesn't require the participation of everyone in a congregation in that specific mission—after all, there is a diversity of gifts. At the same time, it happens because of the shared, joyful compassion of some doing mission for the sake of mission (not for the sake of becoming a legend).

Consider your longings and yearnings. God plants within each human heart longings to help with a specific, concrete mission. Study your Bible. Look at your community. Be in prayer.

I know congregations who are a legend in the community for their help with those who struggle with alcoholism. I know congregations who are a legend for their mission with preschool children, and other congregations for their work with people in early retirement.

I know congregations who are a legend for reaching new Christians with the compassion of Christ. And there are congregations who are legendary for reaching out to their community's homeless citizens.

There is a variety of gifts. There is a variety of ways in which mission is shared, and there is the same, one Lord who abides in it all, who unites these several missions in the gospel.

Congregations can start making their help legendary when they focus on a specific mission, build on their principal strengths, and concentrate the specific resources they share. As they concentrate on that singular mission, two things happen: They deliver concrete help, and they develop their strengths for further mission.

Most congregations who share mission well emphasize one, two, or perhaps three major mission priorities. They do these extraordinarily well. To be sure, they're involved in a wide range of mission activities. Still, they concentrate some of their best leadership and resources on the one to three major priorities.

Because there is a variety of gifts, not everyone in the congregation is asked to serve, for example, preschool children. It is a major priority of the whole congregation in terms of leadership, staffing, funding, outreach, and facilities. And yet only a modest group of people in the congregation may actually be involved sharing that mission well.

In this way the congregation achieves four significant accomplishments:

- It has a major mission priority.
- It encourages people to live out the mission to which God is inviting them.

- It is not making every mission possibility a major mission priority every year.
- It has learned to do some things in mission extraordinarily well. It has learned to focus.

DISCOVERING THE INTERCONNECTEDNESS OF MISSION

As your congregation focuses its mission on a specific human hurt and hope, a life stage, a relational or vocational grouping, or a societal concern, they will be led by God to discover links among all four. One congregation, for example, was sharing an extraordinary mission with families who had children in primary school and discovered that the societal concern about education for these children was a major community problem.

Another congregation's mission with people in poverty led them to a second mission with preschoolers in their community who were living in abject poverty. Their mission grew to include a life stage along with a societal concern.

While sharing a mission with people who are in divorce recovery, we might discover single-parent families with preschoolers in our community who are living in poverty, or nearly so, and thus discover a compelling mission with these families.

We frequently find ourselves sharing mission with people in more than one of the four areas discussed in this chapter. And these missions have integrity and wholeness.

As we share mission and become people of deep prayer and compassion, we trust that God will lead us to new discoveries.

A CONGREGATIONAL RESPONSE
FOR THE INCARNATION

Hope is stronger than memory.

We are the People of Hope.

The cradle of Bethlehem is stronger
           than the thrones of kings.

We are the People of Bethlehem.

The newborn Savior is stronger than
           the armies of the world.

We are the People of New Life.

Light is stronger than darkness.

We are the People of Light.
We are the Christmas People.
We are the People of Wonder and Joy.

3:

Growing Your Mission

But while the young son was yet a long way
off, his father saw him, and had compassion,
and he ran. *Luke 15:20*

COMPASSION AND COMMUNITY

Mission grows with compelling compassion and a deep
sense of community. Compassion gives mission tenderness.
As you share your mission be aware of that profound yearning that led you to it. Sense the community—get to know,
fall in love with, the people you are serving. Community
gives mission kindness.

Don't share in mission merely out of duty or obligation.
Share it with a sense of wonder and joy, a spirit of grace
and love. While people are yet a long way off, run to them
with compassion, as the father did to the prodigal son.

Yes, the other motivations (challenge, reasonability,
and commitment) have served longtime Christians well,
particularly when going to church was the thing to do. In
this time of mission, I invite you to discard that old phrase
"What we need is people with more commitment." A better

choice these days is "What we need is people with more compassion."

Compassion and community are qualities that initially draw people to the Christian movement. When they see examples of compassion, they discover the grace of God and the giving, loving spirit of a congregation. In community they discover roots, place, and a sense of belonging.

A refocus on compassion and community reminds members, key leaders, and pastors that these very qualities drew them to Christ. They in turn are then able to offer these gifts to people new to the Christian movement. The congregation develops a renewed emphasis on compassion in its mission and its future.

Mission happens in the world. That's where we share our compassion and the strengths of community. The mission field is not the congregation. The mission is not the church buildings. It's not the committee meetings. We are invited by God to be a mission outpost to people beyond the church walls.

When we focus inward, we take care primarily of ourselves. Taking care of us is not the mission. Indeed, the irony is that as we lose ourselves in mission we discover that we've done the best job of taking care of ourselves—without trying to do so. In mission we live beyond ourselves.

PRAYER AND SCRIPTURE

Prayer gives mission courage. Undergird your mission with prayer. Ask God to bless the mission, to bless those being helped, to nurture the best within you.

Diligently pray that people's lives will be advanced, that the character and quality of life in the community will be improved, that the cause of peace and justice in the world will move forward, that people will discover Christ more fully as they both share and receive mission. Invite prayer teams in your congregation to pray frequently for the mission's effectiveness.

Scripture gives mission direction. Let your mission draw on and be informed by the resources of the Bible. Study the Christian mission across the centuries. We learn from our beginnings. We learn from studying the Scriptures and from the church's history. Armed with this knowledge, we bring our best wisdom and common sense to the mission.

In this way your mission can be kept simple and straightforward. It can be realistic and achievable, not grandiose and unattainable. Yes, we will be stretched to share our best, and yet our mission will not be so high-flown as to be overwhelming.

Let your mission not be based on the latest fad or trend. Base it on more than graphs and charts, data and demographics. Use statistics and data for information; use Scripture for inspiration and direction.

Don't fall victim to the "fill-in-the-gap" approach to mission. Some people look at the statistical data about their congregation and discover an age range they are missing. Alarmed, they decide that this age range should be the target for their mission. But many strong, healthy congregations do not include people in every age group from the cradle to the grave. Many congregations in Florida, Arizona, and New Mexico, for instance, have few people under sixty-five years of age. This is natural and no cause for concern, because the communities themselves have few people under sixty-five.

Congregations who are building effective mission develop a simple plan that takes seriously their community and the world. Their mission is built on a foundation of prayer and Scripture, wisdom, and common sense.

HEALTH AND HOPE

Some people build strong, healthy congregations. Some build congregations that become weak. Some people build dying congregations.

Weak and dying congregations haven't gotten that way because of someone's laziness, indifference, or apathy. Most weak or dying congregations have a number of people who are working very hard, but they are investing their efforts in the wrong things. Their energy is going toward the things that used to work in a churched culture and no longer work.

Occasionally, of course, decline occurs because of outside causes beyond a congregation's control. When a major industry closes, for instance, an entire town may be virtually shut down. The area then experiences a huge population exodus. Congregations in these situations may lose key leaders, who must move elsewhere to find work.

God doesn't close one door without opening another. Build the mission on the health God gives you. When you do this, both the mission and the health grow stronger. When the mission withers, the health withers. We are given health and life so that we might serve God's mission.

Health grows health. Focus on nurturing and encouraging health and life. This will build a strong mission, which in turn will help people develop a healthy life with their family and their work. Your healthy mission helps others advance healthy lives of wisdom and vision, compassion and generosity, caring and thoughtfulness, and joy and hope.

Build on hope. Hope is stronger than memory. Memory is strong. Hope is stronger. With hope, you know that some of your best years in mission are before you, and you shift your focus from where you have been to where you are heading.

New people in our congregations can participate only in the future; they can't participate in the past. Indeed, none of us can.

We have this confidence: God goes before us, leading us toward that future which God is preparing for us. God gives us hope and strength for the mission.

We have this assurance: We are the Easter people, the people of hope.

A MISSION THAT IS FREELY SHARED

Share the mission as a gift. Attach no conditions or stipulations. There is no, "If you do this, then I will do that for you." There is no bargaining. There are no trade-offs. The mission is freely, generously given as a gift, in the same way that God freely gave his Son for our sake.

Indirect forms of mission, such as sending money to a mission group elsewhere, are helpful because they enable those people to carry out effective mission where they are. From Christianity's earliest days, indirect forms of mission have been important and decisive.

At the same time, it is central to our own health and well-being to participate in some form of direct mission, where we are in personal contact with those being helped. The gift of mission invites personal interaction and involvement. Our direct forms of mission help us to see the urgency and importance of indirect forms of mission. When we don't participate in direct mission, indirect forms of mission become remote and impersonal.

Share the mission in an open way. As you help, invite those you are helping to become part of the mission team. Let the mission be inclusive and reciprocal, not top-down, paternalistic, maternalistic. Just as our lives touch theirs, their lives touch our lives; we benefit and grow mutually.

In a mission that is freely shared, mutual, and open, it may not be entirely clear as to who is really helping whom. Those receiving help are also helping us to live our best. Through participating in the mission, we discover that we too are helped.

FOCUS AND DIRECTION

Your mission will grow best with focus and direction. We usually face the temptation to try to do too much, too soon, in too many directions. We sometimes allow our compulsiveness about perfection to overcome our common sense. Aim for progress, not perfection. It's not wise to try to do everything. Making choices helps develop a focus.

When we allow ourselves to be drawn first this way and then that, we become like Alice, who said to the Cheshire cat, "Which road shall I take?" The cat replied, "Where are you headed?" "I don't know." "Then, it won't matter what road you take." We see many roads and cannot choose among them, so we end up trying to take them all.

Perhaps we shy away from choosing a focus because we don't want to exclude anyone. A church will say, "Oh, but we can't focus our primary mission on children and their families. What about the youth and senior adults?" Take the long look. The stronger and more competent our mission with children and their families is, the more likely we are eventually to develop an effective mission with youth and senior adults.

Strength grows strength. As we discern the primary mission God is inviting us to, we are in a solid position to stay focused. Over time, our mission will become stronger.

Strong, healthy mission congregations are always living at the edge of their resources. They are not conserving, holding, protecting, preserving their resources. They give away what they have, knowing that God will supply resources sufficient to do their mission.

Confident in the direction of their mission, they value the resources God gives them. They are intentional about the resources they share. As you implement your mission plan, monitor your efforts to be sure you are sharing concrete, effective help, not simply good intentions or wishful thinking.

When mission has focus and direction, people are genuinely helped. There is action, not study. There is movement, not meetings. Your mission grows out of objectives that are specific, measurable, concrete, and tangible.

People like to do things that are specific and concrete. It is not true that churches tend simply to keep building buildings. Given a choice between a specific, concrete blueprint for a building and a vague, general mission statement, they will build the building. Given a specific, concrete blueprint for mission, a tangible mission action plan, they will do the mission—and then build whatever buildings serve it. People want to help in ways that actually have an effect, that respond to a specific human need.

At the same time, we must guard against sharing too much help. Too much might in fact be harmful by creating a pattern of dependency or codependency.

Grow your mission with focus and direction. Invest some of your best resources, volunteers, leaders, staffing, and financial support in the mission to which God is calling you. Not all of your resources will be needed for it. You'll use some of your resources in other ways. Still, your mission deserves some of your very best resources.

Be equally intentional about the forms of help you do not offer. No one can help everybody with everything. Decide what you do best, what God has given you the gifts and competencies to do, and share those.

MISSION AND PROGRAM LINKAGE

One of the simplest, best ways you can focus and direct your resources—volunteers, leadership, staffing, and giving—is to create a mission and program linkage. This means building a mission in the community and a program in the church that reinforce each other.

A specific mission always has its focus with people in the community and the world. A church program usually exists to serve church members. It is possible to expand an existing inside-the-church program into the community. If, for example, your church program is geared toward serving elementary-age children and their families, your linking program in the community may be to develop an excellent after-school program. Thus mission and program coalesce. If your after-school program primarily serves families inside the church, it will not be a mission. The link is created when you offer a high-quality program that serves families in the community as well.

Some congregations have a valuable mission with families of preschoolers in the community. But if the major program in the church primarily serves senior adult members, there is no link between the mission focus and program focus.

Churches rarely have the resources required to continue serving in divergent areas equally well. When resources are limited, you can maximize their effectiveness when you invest some of your best resources through linking mission with program.

Consider what kind of mission you can develop to match your program, one that would gain respect and a solid reputation for being the best of its type in the community. Whether it be a preschool, a day care center, a place for scouts or for senior adults, or something else, be sure to keep it specific.

PACE AND TIMING

A second way to focus your resources is to share your mission efforts with a sense of pace and timing, interspersing some strategically timed short-term projects with your longer-term plans. Consider these possibilities:

One time: Some of the best sharing of mission happens through one-time projects. A mission team will join together to build a house or a health clinic. A mission team will sponsor a one-time workshop to assist single parents. With thoughtful planning churches might host a series of one-time events.

Seasonal: A community-wide vacation Bible school each summer serves a whole community of children. A work project each Christmas serves the poor in a city. A community-wide, seasonal seminar helps sixth graders and their families with the transition into the life stage of junior high.

Short term: A seminar for the community consisting of three to five sessions can help families in grief, for instance. A work team can assist in a neighborhood cleanup over three to five Saturdays.

Long term: A mission project becomes long term as it extends over six or more sessions.

Weekly or monthly year round: A few mission projects happen steadfastly on a year round basis, such as weekly day care, or a monthly soup kitchen.

You will involve more people in your mission if you offer more one-time, seasonal, and short-term opportunities along with your long-term and year-round projects.

The numbers in Table 3.1 are meant to represent the proportional distribution of pace and timing that will help you focus your resources for mission.

You can offer eight one-time possibilities, six seasonal, and four short-term for every two long-term and one weekly, year round.

Table 3.1

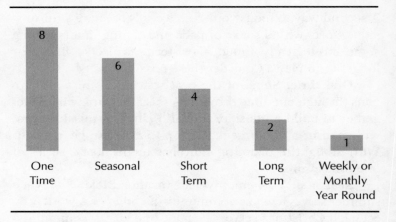

One congregation, for example, felt called to a primary mission with school-age children and their families. They prayerfully and thoughtfully considered their resources and put them toward a series of one-time, seasonal, and short-term mission projects. Each mission project, while distinct, contributed directly to their mission with the families.

Some of the best people to have serving on one-time, seasonal, and short-term mission teams are what we call excellent sprinters. They do everything in highly intensive ways near the time at hand, in quick bursts of energy. They will respond in extraordinary ways to the immediate projects.

Other people, by contrast, are solid marathon runners, working steadily over the long haul. They help with the long-term and weekly or monthly year round mission projects. They may also respond to some of the one-time, seasonal, and short-term mission efforts.

You will gather more volunteers, leaders, mission teams, and giving as you create a series of constructive projects that serve your specific mission. Churches can make a serious mistake if they offer mission possibilities that require only long-term parrticipation. A diversity of projects maintaining a focus on your mission will help keep your resources for mission well centered.

RANGE OF RESOURCES

A third way you can focus your resources is to have a clear sense as to the range of resources you plan to share, and the ones you intentionally plan not to share.

Prayer, for example, constitutes an excellent mission. Praying is one of the best things we do as Christians. A mission prayer team can pray for the specific families served in mission in the community. Their prayers can be helpful in times of both celebration and tragedy or hardship as well as in everyday life. Because people frequently walk through the valley of the shadow, sometimes the best support a church's mission team can offer is prayer.

The mission resource can be motivation, helping people to grow and develop their gifts and competencies. Frequently, people know what they need to decide, and they know the strengths which they have. What benefits them is the motivation to decide and to move forward.

The mission resource can be education, helping people with the facts, knowledge, and insights that advance their well-being as persons. It is worth noting that education is education, not motivation. Some make the mistake of assuming that the more education the more motivation. No, they are distinct. Indeed, some have all the education available; what they need help with is the motivation to decide.

Some families benefit from a mission of fellowship. The loneliness and alienation of our times presses in upon many families with young children, for instance. A preschool support group that works at a deeper level of support and caring can be very valuable.

Another specific mission could be the offering of referrals. The mission team develops the gift for pointing families to the resources in the community that best match their needs. This is shared in the spirit of direct, personal help.

Table 3.2 will help you plan the mission resources you and your congregation can share best in the immediate, midrange, and long-term future. Equally important, the chart helps you to decide the resources you plan *not* to share.

Congregations who build on the gifts God gives them and who have a clear sense of which resources they want to share develop effective missions and healthy congregations. If you disperse your resources in too many directions, you squander the gifts God gives you. Use your resources well, and God will give you more.

DEVELOPING A WHOLISTIC LONG-RANGE PLAN

A wholistic mission plan ensures that all of its components head in the same direction and are not scattered in multiple directions. It has a sense of balance, a "whole cloth" integrity. This kind of long-range plan informs and shapes a congregation's shepherding, worship, groupings, and leadership.

You are encouraged to pray and puzzle, share and discuss, and finally decide a mission action plan which includes your specific key objectives linked with these areas. Equally important, decide where you are *not* headed in these areas.

Table 3.2 Resources Chart

	Immediate	Midrange	Long Term
Prayer			
Motivation, inspiration			
Education, information			
Fellowship, sharing			
Support, caring			
Referral resources			
Crisis intervention			
Short-term help			
Short-term, intensive help			
Long-term help			
Long-term, intensive help			

Then, on the basis of this mission action plan and its program linkages, decide what implications it has for land, landscaping, parking, space and facilities, and giving development.

The best mission plan looks three to five years ahead in most areas of mission; five to seven years ahead in some areas. In a few matters, such as land and buildings to support the mission, the plan may look seven to thirty years ahead.

You can create a wholistic plan using the process described in the book *Twelve Keys to an Effective Church*, the most widely used way of doing long-range mission planning among congregations across the planet. You can do this process effectively on your own, or you can benefit from a trained and experienced Twelve Keys consultant. The art is to develop a plan with realistic objectives, leadership, staffing, and dates.

You might, for example, consider a mission plan that revolves around relational groupings, not just in the church, but in the community. A significant relational grouping is one that gives people a sense of roots, place, sharing, caring, family, home. Each group shares a multiplicity of resources, and yet each has a central focus that serves as the group's primary reason for being. Some groups have been organized to serve new Christians, as a Bible study, or for prayer and spiritual growth. Some groupings have been organized to serve a specific mission, life stage, or recovery process. It might be a group devoted to promoting literacy or one serving families of preschool children.

Mission congregations create groupings for the community as well as groupings for their members. Only congregations in the bygone churched culture could afford to focus solely on church members. Think about how many new groupings you might start in the coming three to five years to serve persons in mission.

LEADERSHIP AND STAFFING

A wholistic mission plan assesses what leadership resources and staffing will best advance the strength and health of the mission. You might decide that a major priority is *basic mission leadership development* with new Christians, transfer members, recent members (four years or less), long-term members, and constituents.

Because we are working in a new age—an age of mission—we need to cultivate leaders who are skilled at mission rather than "church" leadership. Many of us know enough about how to do leadership inside the church. Developing the basic qualities for leadership for our mission in the world is the direction in which we need to head.

You might decide *advanced mission team training* in one or more of these areas is central to your future:

- mission
- visitation
- worship and music
- new groupings
- education
- early childhood development
- administration and finance
- a specific program area

The best training is motivational and educational, inspirational and informational. Group settings such as mission projects, retreats, seminars, workshops, and revivals will augment home study. Many training events are short term and highly intensive, while others are long term.

Decide what kind of future staffing you need for your mission. This might be volunteer, part-time, or full-time. Having a competent staff is decisive for your mission.

Consider what staffing will be important in

- mission and outreach
- shepherding and visiting
- music and worship
- groupings, education, recreation, program
- administration, support, and finance
- maintenance and landscaping

You may not need staffing in all of these areas. At the same time, don't make the mistake of overbuilding and understaffing. Too many churches build too much building and have too little staff. It's better to overstaff and under-build than it is to understaff and overbuild. A strong, competent staff will figure out how to make underbuilt facilities work, but too much building and too little staff means much of the building sits idle much of the time.

Create a balance of pastoral/program staff and secretarial support. I find that too many pastoral/program staff are doing secretarial work. This costs the church more and is less effective. If you have the right secretarial support, the work gets done more quickly and efficiently and is less expensive. If you have only one secretary, whether volunteer, part-time, or full-time, your mission will be served best when that person has strong administrative skills.

Help all areas of your congregation's mission and life reinforce one another. Your mission action plan has balance and integrity as it informs and shapes where you are heading in shepherding, worship, groupings, leadership, and staffing.

A CHECKLIST FOR YOUR MISSION ACTION PLAN

The criteria in Table 3.3 can help you assess the wisdom, strength, simplicity, and value of your congregation's mission action plan.

Table 3.3 Our Mission Action Plan

	Yes	No	Somewhat
1. Advances compassion and community			
2. Builds on prayer and Scripture			
3. Encourages health and hope			
4. Is freely shared, mutual, open			
5. Has focus and direction			
6. Links mission and program			
7. Has pace and timing			
8. Shares an intentional, helpful range of resources			
9. Expands current strengths, adds new strengths			
10. Matches our community and our mission field			
11. Matches the leadership we have and plan to develop			
12. Is wholistic and integrative			

4:

Four Futures
for Congregations

For I was hungry and you gave me food, I was
thirsty and you gave me drink, I was a stranger
and you welcomed me, I was naked and you
clothed me, I was sick and you visited me, I was
in prison and you came to me. *Matt. 25:35–36*

THE APPEAL OF CONGREGATIONS,
NOT INSTITUTIONS

People join a congregation, not a denomination. The surge
of interest in religion and things of the Spirit is connecting
with congregations who behave as mission congregations,
but it is not connecting with churches that behave as de-
nominational institutions. The day of institutional denomi-
nationalism is over. The day of mission movements has
come.

Mission congregations—mission movements—show
their compassion in their lead questions: Who are we serving in the name of Christ? Will this help people in their lives
as gospel, as good news? The driving focus is service with
genuine caring and compassion.

The popularity of house churches, small groups, self-help groups, and interest groups reveals a trend toward informal movements that are more missional than institutional. Indeed, the rise in the number of mega churches is part of the trend toward mission movements.

People are drawn to congregations that are legends on the community grapevine for their specific mission in the community. They do not look in the yellow pages for a specific institutional church to return to. They're not coming *back* to church—they never attended in the first place.

They are drawn to the congregation that is sharing concrete, effective help in a specific mission with them or with someone they know or that is the legend in the community. Life is short. People look for a congregation that doesn't take three months to make a thirty-dollar decision. The bureaucratic traits that have crept into some of the aspects of our churches have become a turnoff to many. It is said a bureaucracy either wears you out or waits you out. Many people choose not to fight it. They simply avoid it, they leave, or they never come.

Find ways to reduce your bureaucratic baggage. If you ordinarily take three months to make a decision, see if you can do it in three weeks, or three days. Streamline the procedures. Reduce the policies. Simplify the regulations. Do not *re*structure; develop *less* structure.

Turn two-hour discussion meetings into twenty-minute decision sessions. A mission field calls for improvisation and creativity. Focus on action more than coordination, the whole more than the parts, progress more than perfection.

Place the real authority with the grass roots, "as close to the coal face" as possible, as close to the front lines as possible, as close to the mission teams as possible. The structures of a mission movement are relative, not absolute; dynamic and flexible, not static and rigid; local, not hierarchical; connected, not centralized; missional, not institutional.

Decide, resolve, determine—today—to take the steps to (re)create a mission movement. Move toward being a mission congregation rather than an institutional church. People long to participate in a mission movement that is growing and building people's lives and destinies.

FOUR FUTURES

In order for congregations to live out their mission, they needn't be huge. It's not always desirable or possible for a congregation to be a mega church.

Don't be infatuated with bigness. Bigger is not necessarily better. God invites us to share a mission that matches our strengths—the strengths with which God has blessed us. Strengths are more important than size. The art is to grow a strong mission, not necessarily a large congregation. Discover the primary mission future toward which you are headed. Build toward your future based on your strengths.

There are four possible futures for congregations:

- mega
- large, regional
- middle
- small and strong

Each of these is marked by a distinctive way of thinking and behaving, and any one of them can apply to a healthy congregation that has a strong mission vision.

Mega Congregations

A mega congregation delivers

- nine of the twelve central characteristics of an effective church with extraordinary strength and excellence

- a compelling mission in the community
- multiple, dynamic services of worship
- a dynamic of creativity and flexibility
- the continuity of an extremely competent staff, key leaders, and a pastor who work well together as a mission team
- a streamlined dynamic of action and momentum
- sufficient space and facilities for the mission without overwhelming debt

Many people mistakenly believe that mega congregations are built single-handedly by a charismatic pastor. To be sure, the pastor often does serve as the public person for the church. But when one looks more closely at healthy mega congregations, one discovers an excellent mission team of leaders, staff, and pastor.

You can count on the growth of many mega congregations in the years to come. They'll be found in a wide range of communities, not simply in larger metropolitan areas.

And know this: The future of the Christian movement does not rest solely on mega congregations. The three other configurations—large and regional, middle, small and strong—are equally important. Of these, the two most productive futures are as a large, regional congregation or as a small and strong congregation. It's toughest to be a middle congregation.

Large, Regional

A large, regional congregation delivers

- nine of the twelve central characteristics of an effective church in strong ways
- an extended regional mission outreach

- the capacity to serve many persons in the community
- one excellent mission-program linkage with continuity
- the continuity of strong key leaders, pastor, and staff who see themselves as a mission team in the community
- many groupings, with new groupings starting each year
- sufficient space and facilities without overwhelming debt

In the final analysis, there is no such thing as a large church. A large church is a collection of smaller congregations who have just enough in common to share the same mission, leadership team, pastor, staff, and facilities. Note that I did not say they have a whole lot in common. They have just enough in common. The art of leading a large, regional congregation is much like leading a cluster of many small congregations.

Small and Strong

Note that I am not saying "small but weak" or "small and dying." Small can be strong, and there are many small congregations that prove this. They build their strengths even if they can't always increase their size. Many are exceptionally strong mission outposts.

Strength is different from size. Even large or mega congregations can be weak or dying. Size alone does not guarantee strength and dynamic leadership.

A small, strong congregation delivers

- nine of the twelve central characteristics of an effective church in a way that contributes to a strong sense of community
- one excellent mission in the area (this overcomes any tendency to be preoccupied with survival)

- a solid spirit of self-reliance and self-sufficiency
- the capacity to draw on community resources to supplement the leadership resources in the congregation
- the continuity of competent, compassionate leaders who see themselves as a mission team
- service to a specific neighborhood—it may be a relational, vocational, sociological, and/or geographical neighborhood
- just enough space and facilities (such as a house church or rented facilities or an owned building), but not so much that it becomes a burden

Churches in the Middle

I've saved the middle congregations for last because it's the most difficult future to do successfully. Some think of the middle as a plateau, but it's really tougher than that. Being in the middle is like five of us deciding we will sing the *Messiah* as a community musical offering. Or being in the middle is like seven of us forming a team to play in the Superbowl against the eleven best players in the NFL.

Middle congregations get beat both ways. They get battered about from both sides. Middle is too large to deliver the intimacy found in a small, strong congregation and not large enough to deliver the mission outreach, resources, staffing, and program of a large, regional congregation.

Leaders and pastors of middle-sized congregations frequently feel battle fatigued, bleary eyed, and worn out. One reason for this is because they are trying to do the middle without the resources their larger counterparts have.

No one of these futures is necessarily easy. To do small and strong or large, regional is difficult enough. To do the middle well is really difficult.

Still, the middle can be done well when these distinctive qualities and behavior patterns are solidly in place:

- nine of the twelve central characteristics of an effective church done with strength and excellence
- one superb mission-program linkage that is the best in the community
- three or more major significant relational groupings in leadership
- the continuity of talented, compassionate leaders, pastor, and staff who see themselves as a mission team
- the capacity to keep focused on the 20-percenters which deliver 80 percent of the results
- the flexibility of a mission-driven structure
- not too many buildings or too much debt

Healthy middle congregations have three or more major leadership groupings. Regrettably, many middle congregations are two-cell churches—the old-timers and the newcomers. The newcomers may not be that new—they may have come thirty years ago. But from the vantage point of the old-timers, they are new. The most common thing a two-cell church does is fight. No one in the community is drawn to a two-cell church fight.

Healthy middle congregations have learned the ability to keep focused on a few key "20-percenters." The basic principle is: 20 percent of the things a group does delivers 80 percent of its accomplishments and achievements; 80 percent of the things a group does delivers 20 percent of its accomplishments and achievements. This is critical to make the middle work. Too many middle congregations become preoccupied with 80-percenters which only deliver 20 percent of the results. Middle congregations tend to become easily distracted, try to do too much for too many, and end up not doing very much very well for anyone.

Healthy middle congregations have developed the flexibility of a mission structure rather than the routine of an institutional structure. They have a modest number of volunteers and leaders, and so they deploy them flexibly and wisely in their mission.

The middle congregation is usually understaffed. Frequently it is carrying too much debt and/or has too many buildings to be able to expand its mission outreach, future staffing, and program.

CLAIMING YOUR DISTINCTIVE QUALITIES

Each type of church—mega; large, regional; small and strong; and middle—has distinctive qualities that are lived out in both the way these congregations think and in their behavior patterns. Small and strong congregations think and act in a manner different from large congregations.

If we were forming a new congregation today, we could decide in the very beginning whether our intent was to become a small and strong congregation or a large, regional congregation. We could make that decision before we had hardly any people. And from the first day onward, we could behave, live, and plan for the future we chose even though we didn't yet have the numbers for it. We could see ourselves in the distinctive way that is characteristic of that future.

Perception yields behavior; behavior yields destiny. We could put into place, from the very beginning, the way of thinking and the behavior pattern that is appropriate to the mission future we have chosen.

I'm not suggesting that it's easy to develop a new congregation—of any kind. At same time, it's easier when you know and claim the future toward which you are headed.

Unfortunately too many new congregations who plan to be large and regional begin by acting like small and strong congregations. If they are able to grow beyond that, they then have to unlearn the distinctive behaviors of the small congregation. If they take up the middle church's behavior pattern, they will again need to unlearn that in order to develop the characteristics appropriate to a large, regional congregation. With all of these nearly imperceptible barriers, it is all too easy to settle in rather than move beyond. And if the continuity of leaders with vision is disrupted, that final barrier becomes the linchpin.

Many large, regional congregations started with small numbers. But from the very beginning they thought, acted, and planned as though they were already large. They more quickly put into place the distinctive qualities of that future and therefore achieved that behavior pattern without having to unlearn earlier behaviors.

Sometimes a large, regional congregation acquires a pastor, several leaders, and staff members who behave as if it were a middle congregation. Given time, that congregation ends up becoming a middle—they muddle to the middle.

A new congregation may plan its future to be small and strong. It will do well so long as it behaves accordingly. But if it begins to imitate the behavior of a middle or a large, regional congregation, it confuses itself. It loses its distinctive qualities. And, more often than not, the result is that it becomes a small, weak congregation.

The best way forward is for a congregation to claim its future and act in correspondence with that goal. It will develop the strengths and qualities central to its identity and mission, and God will bless its mission.

PERSONS SERVED IN MISSION

All four futures succeed best as they focus on mission, as they center on the number of persons served in mission.

Mission-driven congregations, mission-driven movements, when they do think of size, focus on the size of the mission rather than the size of the membership.

Think mission numbers before you think member numbers. This is a mission field. Strong, healthy congregations in all four futures focus on serving persons through mission.

Paul said, "Be ye transformed by the renewing of your mind." As people wrestle with the future, they try to quantify concepts, to attach numbers to them. In our time—a time of mission—we need a renewing of our minds. The key number is not how many people are members. The key number is persons served in mission.

In healthy congregations that are mission driven, the progression often works like this: Persons are first served in mission; then some of these begin to worship with us; and then some become part of the mission team.

Mission congregations, and mission movements, when they keep statistics, keep track of the number of persons served in mission who have been helped during the past year. They set mission objectives for the number they plan to serve in mission during the coming year.

We still have too many congregations who track only membership and internal participation. They set membership objectives for the coming year. People keep track of the statistics that are important to them. Statistical categories reveal their real theology.

It is encouraging to note that several of the major mission movements are increasingly tracking the numbers of persons served in mission. Likewise they are setting mission objectives for the numbers of persons they plan to help in the coming year.

When we perceive congregational size and strength in comparison with all other congregations in the country, and, for that matter, across the world, statistically most congregations are in fact larger and stronger than they think they are. People think of size in relation to context, and they tend to measure size according to the context with which they are familiar. In a churched culture the defining number was how many members a church had. On a mission field the defining number is how many persons served in mission have been helped with their lives and destinies in the name of Christ.

Given the future you are envisioning for yourself, the best wisdom is to focus on the distinctive qualities and behavior patterns you want to be present in your congregation.

HEALTHY CONGREGATIONS AND THEIR FACILITIES

Mission shapes mortar. Across the centuries of the Christian movement, many congregations have understood their calling to be to build the mission, not to build buildings.

In our time many healthy congregations around the planet who are sharing God's mission don't own a building! They would be distracted from their mission if they got involved in constructing, caring for, and maintaining a building.

Many congregations go a long time without a building, and some never build space and facilities. Some are house churches. Some rent or lease space and facilities. They are so involved in their mission that they don't have time to build buildings. They are mission driven, not building driven.

Mortar follows mission, not the reverse. Whatever your strengths or numbers, think a long time before you build buildings. Build the mission. Then, if need be, rent or lease a building. As a last resort, build a building.

Our church buildings have sometimes been a reflection of our culture. The art is to let whatever buildings you use reflect the mission more than the culture. Castle owners construct cathedrals. Homeowners build church buildings. Let mission shape mortar.

Small, strong congregations tend to have almost enough facilities to share their mission well. Small and weak or small and dying congregations tend to have more space and facilities than they need, and, regrettably, the maintenance of the building ends up being their primary mission.

Healthy large, regional congregations tend to build sufficient facilities to serve their mission. A regional congregation that is weak or dying has usually underbuilt. They end up with insufficient space to carry out a strong regional mission. Ultimately the absence of adequate facilities suffocates their mission.

Weak or dying middle congregations tend to have accumulated a combination of not quite enough space and facilities, too much debt, and not enough staff. The lack of adequate space, coupled with too much debt, greatly hinders them. The debt, in their perception, blocks them from having enough competent staff, and they end up not being able to share their mission well.

Consider first your mission, build and strengthen it; then envision how that mission can be carried out in the space and facilities you have.

On occasion we find a congregation that has gradually shifted its identity toward its buildings and away from its mission. They may have developed an architectural master plan that is displayed on a wall for everyone to see. Over many years they have worked to establish their buildings— first stage one, then stage two, and finally stage three of the plan. When the master plan is completed, the congregation finds itself in an identity crisis. If its self-definition has been wrapped up in constructing buildings and paying for them for such a long time, any original vision of mission will have been long since forgotten.

Mission-driven congregations have a mission action plan—a "blueprint for people" focusing on those they plan to help in mission. Over many years they measure their success by the number they serve and the quality of the care they share. They may also build some buildings to serve the mission. At the end of those years their identity is sound, substantial, and enduring because the mission endures.

Table 4.1 Summary of the Twelve Central Characteristics of Effective, Successful Congregations

Relational Characteristics	Functional Characteristics
1. Specific, Concrete Missional Objectives 1 2 3 4 5 6 7 8 9 10	7. Several Competent Programs and Activities 1 2 3 4 5 6 7 8 9 10
2. Pastoral/Lay Visitation in Community 1 2 3 4 5 6 7 8 9 10	8. Open Accessibility 1 2 3 4 5 6 7 8 9 10
3. Corporate, Dynamic Worship 1 2 3 4 5 6 7 8 9 10	9. High Visibility 1 2 3 4 5 6 7 8 9 10
4. Significant Relational Groups 1 2 3 4 5 6 7 8 9 10	10. Adequate Parking 1 2 3 4 5 6 7 8 9 10
5. Strong Leadership Resources 1 2 3 4 5 6 7 8 9 10	11. Adequate Space and Facilities 1 2 3 4 5 6 7 8 9 10
6. Solid, Participatory Decision Making 1 2 3 4 5 6 7 8 9 10	12. Solid Financial Resources 1 2 3 4 5 6 7 8 9 10

5:

Location and Mission

Jesus Christ is the same yesterday and
today and forever. *Heb. 13:8*

MISSION FIRST, BUILDINGS AFTER

Once you have developed your mission action plan—your
blueprint for people—then, and only then, ask yourself two
questions: What is our best long-term location? What land,
parking, space, and facilities do we need to advance our
mission in the community in the coming years?

Before you improve your present space or build new facilities at your present site consider its long-term value to
the mission, looking ten to fifty years ahead.

If you know you're already situated in a poor location,
don't overbuild there. You'll be trapped. Consider seriously
whether you are overbuilding on the present site.

You can also ask yourself, What would be a wise investment for the long-term future of our mission? Will the congregation's leaders fifty years from now feel that we exer-
cised wisdom to stay at the present location?

A congregation may have been at its present location for
a number of years, but this is not a primary reason to stay
there. Many churches I've worked with find out by looking

into their history that their congregation was founded at a particular location in the 1870s, moved in the 1890s, then moved again in the 1920s. Their established pattern is to find a new location when needed. The previous leaders were wise enough to evaluate each location on its merits rather than for any traditional value. In that same spirit it is important for a congregation to evaluate any current location before adding more buildings.

With an overbuilt, poor location, we won't be able to find a buyer who can afford our land and buildings. Any group strong enough to do so will be wise enough to buy a better location and will have the leadership and financial resources for it. We will then find ourselves locked into an unsuitable location.

In business, it is said that three things are vital to successful investment: location, location, and location. In the church the three things that contribute to success are mission, mission, and mission. Yes, a congregation with a compelling, legendary mission can overcome a poor location. It is extraordinarily difficult nevertheless. At the same time, imagine the potential for success if a church has both a compelling, legendary mission and an excellent location. They will be in the strongest position to serve persons in the community in the name of Christ.

Thus when you consider your best long-term location, you will want to evaluate

- your present location and any other possible locations
- the options for staying and moving
- the various ways you can secure an excellent location

LOCATION

Evaluate, prayerfully and thoughtfully, your present site and, for that matter, any future sites you may be considering in terms of these factors:

- location
- mission potential
- property characteristics
- finances

The church site evaluation forms in Tables 5.1, 5.2, 5.3, and 5.4 will give you the basic criteria and specifications for property evaluation, selection, and, as helpful, purchase. Should your congregation be among the many house-church congregations, or should you be renting or leasing facilities, some specifications on the list will apply directly; others will not.

Healthy churches need adequate parking throughout the week. They have a full range of activities—both mission and program—all through the week, not just on Sunday.

As you count parking spaces, know that each space allows for 1.75 persons per car, based on the national average. Congregations with a compelling mission with children and their families may average 2.0, and occasionally 2.25 persons per car.

Congregations who allow themselves to grow old together tend to move from 1.75 down to 1.25 persons per car over the years. They experience a decline in worship attendance even though the parking lot is full because there is a lower average number of persons per car.

Think of the parking in relation to the total number of persons on the site at one time, not in relation to the size of the sanctuary alone.

If you build the minimum parking required to meet the local building code, you will not provide the parking you need. As a result, you will have more sanctuary space than you will ever be able to fill because your insufficient parking limits people's participation.

There is a direct correlation between three elements: parking, worship attendance, and giving. To discover the

Table 5.1 Church Site Evaluation: Location

Criteria and Specifications	Maximum	This Site
1. Major thoroughfares and traffic volume favorable to site	60	
2. Minimal geographic barriers and community boundaries in area	50	
3. Traffic direction patterns toward site	50	
4. Key side of road in relation to traffic patterns going to work and/or going home	30	
5. Geographic visibility: the high side of the road	30	
6. Minimal barriers (natural and buildings) immediately surrounding site	30	
Subtotal	250	

annual giving value of each parking space, divide the total number of parking spaces into the total giving to all causes for the most recent year.

Refer to both *Twelve Keys to an Effective Church* and *Dynamic Worship* for more helpful suggestions on parking. Decide the amount of parking you plan to make available in terms of

- number of parking spaces
- number of turnover parking spaces
- number of persons per car
- convenience of parking locations
- distance of parking from facilities

Consider location in terms of the variety of ways in which you plan to use the land, taking seriously that

Table 5.2 Church Site Evaluation: Mission Potential

Criteria and Specifications	Maximum	This Site
1. Total population density within average trip time[1]	60	
2. Potential for persons served in mission matches congregation's mission	50	
3. Major community concerns and needs in area match congregation's mission	40	
4. Socioeconomic and culture profiles, both a match and diversity with congregation	40	
5. Within average trip time to nearest major community institutions, schools, and recreation programs	30	
6. Within average trip time to nearest comparable, healthy congregations	30	
Subtotal	250	

[1] Average trip time refers to the amount of time people spend traveling (one way) to work, to major social and recreational activities, and to primary shopping areas. It refers to the amount of time spent for an average trip in everyday life. People develop an average trip time horizon in day-to-day life, and they are perfectly willing to drive within their average trip time horizon to be part of a congregation in which they discover compassion and community. People go to the church nearest their heart, not their house.

- it is a finite amount of land
- a balance of uses is central, with no one component over-sized in relation to the others
- a spirit of compassion and a sense of community is what people long for and look for

Because it is finite, the amount of land you have will need to be developed wisely. It is more attractive and less

Table 5.3 Church Site Evaluation: Property Characteristics

Criteria and Specifications	Maximum	This Site
1. Parking availability on-site, off-site[1]	60	
2. Ingress to and egress from property	50	
3. Size and shape of property in relation to immediate and long-term usage	40	
4. Topography, contour, drainage, water table	40	
5. Zoning, setbacks, and long-term development possibilities	30	
6. Aesthetics and beauty of location	30	
Subtotal	250	

[1]The key factor is the availability of parking on the site. Churches can no longer depend on using contiguous parking owned by some business or even on-street parking around the site. That time has gone. Churches must be prepared to be virtually self-sufficient in their parking needs.

expensive to invest in well-landscaped grounds than in limited-use buildings.

Having two or three worship services and two or three church school sessions does require more parking and staff. But this is more effective and less expensive than building the additional church school classrooms needed in order to serve the same number of people with only one church school session.

With respect to balance and community, ask yourself how you plan to use the property to communicate a spirit of compassion and a sense of community. It goes beyond whether the site and facilities are user friendly. Do people experience the relational qualities of compassion and community? Do the buildings, signs, and site evoke and communicate a sense of help, home, hope?

Assess the realistic usability of the land and the ease of accessibility (ingress and egress) of the property. Be sensitive to the shape and contours of the land and the ways these enhance people's discovery of being community together.

Thus, looking farther into the future, consider the amount of land to be invested in

- entrances and exits to the property
- adequate parking
- attractive landscaping and gathering areas
- playgrounds and recreational areas
- worship and music areas
- church school, community life center, and administrative facilities
- maintenance storage, exterior equipment, and miscellaneous spaces

The initial purchase investment should be evaluated in relation to (1) the persons who will be served and (2) the giving return on your initial investment. Another site may have a higher price tag, yet it may enable you to serve more people. Its return on investment in relation to enhancing and expanding the congregation's mission with people could make it a better choice.

A site that costs less to purchase may eventually cost more in terms of lost mission opportunity if you will not be able to serve as many people. The up-front cost may be cheaper, but if it inhibits the ability to serve a range of persons, it is a very costly site.

Return on investment can also be considered in relation to future giving, looking twenty-five to fifty years ahead. A higher-priced site on a main road might be passed over unless put to this test. In the long term, its higher return on investment will help pay for it. Because of greater

Table 5.4 Church Site Evaluation: Financial Considerations

Criteria and Specifications		Maximum	This Site
1. Return on investment in relation to people and giving		110	
2. Usage/purchase alternatives[1]		90	
3. Title to property, easements, deed restrictions		50	
	Subtotal	250	

[1]The usage/purchase alternatives are discussed in depth in the later section on "Ways to Secure an Excellent Location."

visibility and accessibility it has the potential to generate stronger worship participation. The more new people who worship, the higher the giving, and the higher the return on investment.

For example, a $700,000 site on a main road generates strong worship participation thus yielding a giving return averaging $20,000 a year more than would be realized from a site off a main road. Over the course of twenty-five years, this means $500,000 more for the mission.

A site located one or two blocks off a main road may initially appear to cost less at $500,000. But when you consider the lost net new giving, that site actually costs more—the initial $500,000 and the lost new giving of $500,000. Over the long term that supposedly cheaper site costs $1,000,000.

That is an expensive site, and, what is worse, it is the poorer location for twenty-five long, long years. The cheapest purchase price may be the most costly choice in the long run.

Table 5.5 Church Site Evaluation: Summary

Criteria and Specifications	Maximum	This Site
Points from evaluating		
Location	250	
Mission potential	250	
Property characteristics	250	
Financial considerations	250	
Grand Total	1,000	

The strongest location will yield the strongest financial contributions for mission, leadership, staffing, and facilities. It has a greater payback value. The less expensive, weaker location may be cheaper on the front end, but it will not deliver the same strength of mission or the same strength of financial contributions over twenty-five to fifty years.

Therefore compare both the front-end investment and the long-term return in persons served and in giving contributions for the church's mission.

Having completed the church site evaluation forms, you may enter the subtotals on the church site evaluation summary in Table 5.5 to obtain a total score.

With this total score for each site considered, use Table 5.6 to help you visually compare the scores of your current site and any sites under consideration to discover the relative overall strength of each site.

With this evaluation done, you are in a strong position to make informed choices among the best options for your future.

Table 5.6

Strength of Site	Maximum	This Site's Score
	1000	
Excellent site		
	800	
Good site		
	600	
Average site		
	400	
Fair site		
	200	
Poor site		
	0	

THE OPTIONS FOR STAYING AND MOVING

Consider, with prayer and wisdom, all your options before heading too quickly to investing resources in improving or building new facilities at your present location. Keep as many options open as possible. Once you improve and/or build at the present site, you may close the door on some options you might later wish you had available. The options are

1. Stay and go
2. Stay and go ⟶ move
3. Move
4. Secure land at a new location as a wise investment and an "insurance policy" for our long-term future

5. Stay, buy land, develop adequate parking
6. Stay, maximize present facilities
7. Stay, buy land, develop adequate parking, improve current space, build new facilities
8. Stay, secure land to protect our future
9. Sponsor a new congregation
10. Stay and study

Look at all ten. Select six of the ten to study more closely. After you have studied those six, choose four to examine in greater depth. Then, of those four, select three for further, thoughtful consideration for your long-term future, looking ten to fifty years ahead. Finally decide which one option or set of options will best advance your mission.

Stay and Go

We continue at our present location and build new facilities at a new nearby location. So long as the new location is close (within five to seven minutes), this option works well.

One church, on the town square, had a wonderful old sanctuary with extraordinary stained glass windows. They wanted to build a community life center and some additional classrooms to serve the children of the community. There was no more land available on the town square.

They found an excellent site five minutes away. During the week much of the congregation's mission is carried out at the community life center. On Sundays some people go to the church school at the new location, then to worship at the town square sanctuary. I say "new location," and yet they've been doing this for nearly thirty years.

In the stay and go option, there is no intent to move away from the existing site. We simply plan to live out our mission in the community utilizing two locations.

Stay and Go ⟶ Move

In this option we plan to build stage one of our new facilities at our new location. For a specific limited time we plan to use both locations. Then we will build stage two of our new facilities and move to our new location, vacating the first site.

This option works when there is a reasonable, specific date for completing stage two and moving. We may build classrooms and a community life center at our new location, planning initially to use the advantages of both locations. Then in five years (the key is a specific target date, five, seven, ten years ahead) we plan to be fully at the new location.

Move to a New Location

In this option we move to our new location, not gradually as above, but in one step. One Sunday we're at the old location; the next Sunday we're at the new location.

Having moved to the new location, we may build some additional facilities there at some point in the future.

You should be aware that there is no magic in relocating. I know of congregations who were dying at an old location, moved to a new location, and died there. They were not delivering nine of the twelve characteristics of effective churches at the old location, and after moving they did not deliver them at the new location either. There is no merit in moving for the sake of moving.

Having said that, I do want to affirm that many congregations are currently struggling in locations that no longer work for them as they once did. For example, the current location may have originally been on a main road, but because of certain municipal developments, it's now on a relatively inaccessible street. In such instances, the three options just described, and those that follow, are helpful.

Secure Land

We plan to continue at our present location for the foreseeable future. We have no plan to move. Yet we are somewhat uncertain as to the long-term viability of our present site. To protect our future options, we secure another location as an insurance policy, so that we have an alternative location for the future.

This option works very well when the new site is a wise investment. Beware of somebody's "bargain." Purchase an excellent site. Some years from now, if the decision is to continue at the present site, we may be able to sell the new property for a profit, which can be put toward our mission.

Stay, Buy Land, Develop Adequate Parking

Frequently a current location is greatly strengthened by the acquisition of more land to provide adequate parking. Consider the maximum number of persons you hope to have on the site at any one time; then develop sufficient parking spaces to accommodate their cars. See *Twelve Keys to an Effective Church* for fuller resources.

Stay, Maximize Present Facilities

Rather than adding more buildings, consider ways the existing buildings can be more sensibly utilized to expand the mission. Congregations invest much time and money to build new facilities when in fact they would have been better off maximizing the use of their current space. You might add more services of worship or more church school sessions before adding bigger facilities.

Both chapter 6 in this book and chapters 9, 10, and 11 in *Dynamic Worship* will be helpful with this option. This option is frequently used in combination with one or more of the other options.

Stay, Buy Land, and Improve

Be certain to provide for adequate parking before you build further at the current location. Once you have done that, then improve your present facilities and/or build new facilities. Depending on your mission plan, you may want to build new facilities; then improve current facilities; or vice versa. Let your mission shape the sequence.

Stay, Secure Land to Protect the Future

When a congregation already has adequate parking and sufficient facilities, it becomes a wise investment to secure additional land at the present location for two reasons. First, this keeps the options open at the current site. Second, this improves the value of the present site so that should the congregation decide to move at some point in the future, it can be sold easily. Sometimes it is wise to buy land at the present site simply to ensure the viability of the site.

Sponsor a New Congregation

This option is to invest resources to help start a new congregation. We can achieve this option in tandem with several of the others. This plan is particularly helpful for small and strong congregations and large, regional congregations. The leaders of a small congregation, for example, would advisedly think and pray a long time before deciding to build new facilities. They might do better to help start another new small, strong congregation. They can grow the mission well without having to run the risk of overbuilding.

Customarily I advise middle congregations to wait until they have developed the mission and strengths of a large, regional congregation before they consider this option.

Stay and Study

I include this because it is an option congregations frequently choose. Sometimes, albeit in a small number of cases, it does make sense to stand pat, to do nothing, to wait for a better time to decide. There are times when it may be better, for the moment, to do nothing rather than to do the wrong thing. In that sense, this is a viable option.

However, we may do nothing because we have developed analysis paralysis. We may have become simply too sheltered where we are. We may be in a state of denial regarding the long-term viability of the present location. We may be looking for an unrealistic level of certainty in making decisions. Many choices in life have a 60 to 70 percent level of certainty. Few decisions have a 90 percent level of certainty; to wait for that is unrealistic.

Yet in all these instances, by doing nothing we lose the moment. Years later the congregation will be weaker, fewer, grayer, digging deeper and deeper into our pockets to meet a shrinking budget—and we will look back and remember when we were strong enough to have decided and wish we had.

A Set of Options

It is possible that a combination of options is your best way forward. Many congregations feel that their best immediate future is with options 4 and 6, securing land at a better location as a wise investment and as an insurance policy to protect their future, and, for the time being, staying and maximizing their present facilities.

Some congregations do 4, 5, and 6. They secure land at a better location to protect their future, secure an agreement on nearby land to improve their current parking, and maximize their present facilities.

Many congregations do 6 and 9—they both maximize their present facilities and sponsor a new congregation. Some do 5 and 9, securing enough land to guarantee adequate parking and sponsoring a new mission congregation.

Many congregations decide to do 4 and 10, securing land at a new location that serves as a wise investment and, for the time being, actively studying the best options for their future mission.

These ten options are not all mutually exclusive. Some work well together to keep open the future possibilities for your mission. Some others are mutually exclusive—by choosing one of them you automatically exclude some others. Discover which option or set of options will best advance your future.

WAYS TO SECURE AN EXCELLENT LOCATION

Create a land study task force. Authorize it to search out the best possibilities in terms of land, usage and/or purchase alternatives, and arrangements to secure the land. A task force made up of three to five people searches intensively for the best ways forward in the direction the church is moving. Frequently this task force researches the best information on the options just discussed and provides leadership in narrowing down the focus to the best choices.

The task force also eventually secures a contract with the owner of the land and takes it to the appropriate congregational governing body for a decision. The task force does not have authority to sign a contract on behalf of the congregation; it can only secure a negotiated contract that has been signed by the property owner and place it before the congregation. No rules of any church body prohibit an owner of a piece of property from agreeing to sign a contract. The property is, after all, owned by the owner.

Any contract should have the standard "subject to financing" contingency clause. As appropriate, it would also include a "subject to congregational approval" contingency clause.

Following negotiations with the task force, the owner of the property has the right to sign whatever contract makes sense to him or her. Only after the owner has signed a binding contract is it appropriate for the leaders and the congregation to hold discussions about that specific contract. Until the owner signs a contract that locks in the date, price, and terms of the agreement, it is unwise for anyone in the church—the leaders or any official body of the church—to discuss publicly whether to buy any specific piece of property.

Without a binding contract, the property purchase can be undone by one person's unwitting remarks. Too many times I've seen this happen when someone says he can remember when the church could have bought that piece of property for one-fourth the current asking price. Unfortunately, what usually has happened is the owner was offended by unofficial talk and discussions and decided never to deal with that church again. Or the owner may have heard so much grapevine discussion about how badly the church needed that property that she inflated the asking price.

The land study task force might secure a direct purchase contract, or it might secure a contract that confirms one or more of these other usage and/or purchase alternatives:

1. Right of use agreement
2. First right of refusal
3. Option to purchase

4. Rental

5. Short-term lease

6. Long-term lease

7. Gift from owner

8. Gift from interested person

9. Lease-purchase

10. Purchase and lease back

11. Purchase and joint venture

12. Joint venture

13. Undividable interest

14. Third-party purchase, sale to church

15. Land swap

It's not always necessary to purchase a piece of property immediately. The key is to *secure* the property in the most equitable way for both the church and the owner.

In making arrangements to secure the land, the task force works out any of these appropriate specifics:

1. Total price, for rental, lease, or purchase

2. Down payment

3. Front-end money: initial three- to five-year investment

4. Land use and/or acquisition schedule

5. Loan

6. Time of loan

7. Amortization period

8. Payment schedule

9. Interest only and interest/principal payments

10. Balloon payment(s)

11. Interest rate

12. Return on investment projections

It is important that the land study task force take a complete, specific, reasonable, and clear proposal to the appropriate body of the congregation for its consideration.

Decisions on location are most important. It is central to have achieved a thoughtful evaluation of your present location and any possible locations.

Given these evaluations, thoughtfully consider the various ways you can secure an excellent location. Then you will be in the strongest position to decide whether and how to improve your present space, and whether, where, and when to build any new facilities.

A PRAYER FOR FORGIVENESS

God of grace and of galaxies,
        of salvation and solar systems,
      we are grateful for your compassion with us.

The immensity of the universe
      teaches us the immensity
          of your love for us.

Stir our strengths.
      Touch our lives.

The worst of us is in the best of us.
      The best of us is in the worst of us.

Cleanse the worst from within us.
      Forgive our feeble sins.
          Have mercy on our terrible sins.

Nurture the best within us.
      In Christ's name, we pray, amen.

6:

Building Space and Facilities

> Whoever drinks of the water that I shall give him will never thirst; the water that I shall give him will become in him a spring of water welling up to eternal life. *John 4:14*

The factors that help in your deliberations as you consider maximizing your present space, improving it, or building new facilities are

- balance
- flexibility
- something new
- leadership, scheduling, staffing

BALANCE

When considering your present facilities and any future facilities, create a constructive balance between your parking, sanctuary, fellowship hall, and church school space.

There is no balance when you have parking for 300 people and a sanctuary that will seat 500. On special occasions such as Christmas Eve and Easter, you may have 500 in attendance, but on a regular basis the average will range around 300. Either the parking is underbuilt or the sanctuary is overbuilt. It is out of balance.

Or you may have parking for 500 people and a sanctuary that seats 500. Those are in balance. But a fellowship hall that accommodates only 150 is out of balance.

Some have balance in their parking, sanctuary, and fellowship hall—they all provide for 500, but their church school space provides for 200. It is not accidental that their average church school attendance is around 200.

It's not essential for all four components be equal in their capacity. The actual capacities will vary given the church's mission priorities and the weekly and Sunday schedule of programs and activities. For example, we may have parking for 1,000, a sanctuary that seats 500, and church school space for 500. These ratios are in balance when we have worship and church school at the same time, and there are about 500 in worship and 500 in church school.

When we offer two worship services at the same time as two church school sessions, some people go to church school and then to worship, and some go to worship and then to church school. The adequate parking plus the Sunday schedule provide a sense of balance.

Some congregations have parking for 500, a sanctuary for 500, and church school space for 250. They offer church school in both their weekly preschool and after-school program as well as on Sunday. With this strength of programming they create a sense of balance.

It's crucial to build adequate parking for your current facilities before you build anything new. You may need to "increase" your parking by offering multiple services as well.

If your sanctuary is undersized in relation to your church school facilities, develop two or more services of worship before you build a larger sanctuary.

If your fellowship hall is undersized in relation to your other facilities, then for major congregational events rent space in the community or have multiple events that serve the fellowship needs of your congregation. It is possible to create a sense of balance through a constructive combination of rental facilities and multiple events.

FLEXIBILITY

The larger the space, the more flexible its use. Build generous-sized spaces that can accommodate multiple uses, and use any current large space creatively. For example, a room of 700 square feet, 20 by 35, is more likely to be used easily by a weekly preschool program, an after-school program, a variety of other groups through the week, and also on Sunday morning. A smaller space of 300 square feet, 15 by 20, has more limited usage. Three rooms of 300 square feet each gives us 900 square feet of space, but one 700-square-foot room (or whatever expansive size suits your plans) will do the task for all three in a superior way, especially when we are creative in our scheduling and programming. I'd rather use that one generous-sized space three times on Sunday than have three smaller spaces each used once on Sunday. The larger space will be used more fully through the week as well.

Another example: It makes better sense to have one generous-sized space that can serve as a church school classroom, a meeting room, an attractive church parlor, and a bride's room than it does to have four smaller spaces each dedicated to a single use.

Look at your current large spaces and discover the best ways to create flexible, multiple uses of these before you build new space. And when you do build new space, work hard to create multiple uses for the rooms.

If your pledging falls short of the goal, don't shrink the size of the rooms to match the money. Instead build fewer large rooms. One church did this. They had planned to build ten rooms averaging 20 by 35, a total of 7,000 square feet. These rooms were for their weekday preschool, day care, after-school program, evening meetings and groups, Saturday programs, and for Sunday morning and evening. The rooms were to accommodate multiple uses and storage.

They hoped to raise sufficient funds to build all ten. For a variety of reasons, the initial pledging came in short of the goal. They built fewer but adequate classrooms, using a plan that allowed for future expansion. They knew the multiple uses would fill their immediate needs, and the sense of satisfaction from using these flexible spaces would soon generate the momentum and the money needed to add the remaining rooms.

It would have been a mistake to shrink the room size to match the money. They would have ended up with ten smaller rooms. Those less adequate spaces would not have allowed for the multiple uses and the storage needs of the various groupings who hoped to use the space. And a sense of dissatisfaction with the reduced facilities would have lingered and made it more difficult to accelerate the momentum for any future building for a long time to come.

Don't shrink the mission and the facilities to match the immediate money. You'll end up with inadequate rooms and you'll have a hard time raising the enthusiasm and the money to build anything more.

SOMETHING NEW

The older your facilities, the more important it is to show something "new" each year. Occasionally a congregation will let their craving for something nice and new mislead them into an ill-advised building program. It's important to satisfy this desire, but it doesn't need to mean building new facilities. You can accomplish the effect of showing something new through

- ongoing restoration
- landscaping
- signs
- parking

You can develop a long-term plan of ongoing restoration that includes a schedule of refurbishment of specific spaces, preventative maintenance, and emergency repairs. This approach to your buildings will be less expensive and more effective, and it will deliver something new each year.

I work with many congregations whose buildings are decades old and neglected. Each year the sense of depression gets deeper and the cost of restoration or improvements gets higher. My counsel to them is not to fix up everything at once, even if they do have enough money to. If everything were refurbished immediately, things would look really nice for the first year; then the former pattern would repeat itself: twenty-plus years of fade and decline until the next capital improvement campaign.

Too many churches go through the cycle of allowing the buildings to deteriorate and then, when it gets bad enough, initiating a capital improvements campaign to fix everything. Not only is this a costly cycle, it doesn't deliver something new each year. Long periods of declining buildings teach the community and the congregation that this is a declining church.

The best way forward is to put in place an ongoing plan for restoration that looks seven years or more ahead. This is more effective, less expensive, and delivers something new

each year. And it teaches the community and the congregation that we are not a fading church; we are a renewing and
growing congregation.

I worked with one congregation whose buildings were
from the late 1800s. For a variety of reasons the care of the
buildings was neglected from the 1920s to the early 1980s.
We developed a long-range plan so that each year a specific
restored area would coordinate aesthetically with what had
been restored before and what would follow. In the first year
the narthex to the sanctuary and the vestibule to the fellowship hall were refurbished. These were two highly visible
"quick wins" that didn't require a great deal of money.

In the second year the church redid two of the rooms in
the education building—one of the corner rooms (where
many of the groups would meet) and the corner room at the
other end of the building that was used as the nursery. This
is a principle I call "cornering the building." One corner
looks really nice and another corner looks really nice, and
everything in between looks a whole lot worse; we thereby
generate the momentum and the money to continue restor-
ing the rest of the building.

In the third year the church refurbished two more
rooms. In year seven, the major project of the sanctuary was
achieved. In year eight, the church started over.

With an ongoing restoration plan we satisfy people's desire for something new and we don't run the risk of overbuilding. We avoid the image of a declining church, and we
use a less expensive, more effective way to care for our
buildings.

Another area where we can deliver something new is
in our landscaping. Buildings tend to become invisible. The
more your building looks the same out front year after
year, the more it disappears. People drive by without ever
seeing it.

You can have a long-term plan that, step-by-step, includes planting new flowers, trimming the bushes, pruning the trees, adding a new landscaping feature, and creating freshly painted signs. We wouldn't do all of these in one year. We would do these landscaping steps with a long-range plan that helps the building look new each year.

The art is to dress the building with the landscaping. This is more effective and less expensive than creating gingerbread ornamentation, which can be quite expensive.

We can also deliver something new by developing a better parking layout. We can provide easier parking for handicapped persons, and we can develop appropriate parking for visitors. We can create a parking team of greeters, especially for our most crowded Sundays.

In this wide range of ways we can, over a period of years, continue to deliver something new without going to the expense of adding buildings. Even when we do build new facilities, we will still need to have such a long-range plan to satisfy the desire for something new for the years to come.

LEADERSHIP, SCHEDULING, STAFFING

Maximize your current space use with creative leadership, multiple scheduling, and sufficient staffing before you build new facilities. You can invest some of your best money in outstanding staff, leadership, and resources who can build

- church school sessions two or three times on Sunday, for example, at 8:30, 9:30, and 11:00
- after-school church school programming at your site and, as helpful, in one or more nearby elementary schools.

A competent part-time staff person can achieve the sole objective of building an excellent church school at 8:30.

This church school might have a breakfast Bible class, a marriage enrichment class, a forum discussion class. There would be church school for the children of the adults who attend, most likely infants, toddlers, kindergarteners, and first through third graders. Although it would not be a full-blown, cradle-to-grave church school, it would serve a wide range of people who then worship at 9:30.

An equally competent part-time staff person can develop a strong church school at 11:00 as well. Other creative staff members can build an excellent after-school program.

There is no need to try to gather everyone altogether in one hour of church school. The more options you offer, the more people you serve. Investment in competent staff to develop multiple options is more effective and less expensive than building too many facilities that sit empty much of the week.

Likewise an excellent 8:30 choir director builds an excellent 8:30 choir and related music groups and thus a strong 8:30 worship service. The same is true for the 9:30 and 11:00 worship service, and for a worship service during the week.

Even in churches that have a full-time choir director, we bring on board a part-time, extraordinarily competent choir director to build the music for an 8:30 service of worship. We do the same for a worship service offered during the week.

A full-time choir director has as much as he or she can say grace over, building music for one or two worship services. That same individual hardly ever maintains the same strength for three or four services. Thus we build the music staffing that strengthens all of our worship services. You'll find a fuller range of helpful suggestions on this in *Dynamic Worship*.

The basic principle is to find creative ways for leadership, scheduling, and staff to maximize the use of the present facilities before deciding to build any new facilities.

Even when you build new facilities, you will need to build the staffing to maximize their use. New spaces require sound staffing and scheduling if they are to achieve the fullest potential. Invest in competent, compassionate staff, part-time and full-time. This is more effective and less expensive.

The first characteristics of an effective church are the relational ones:

- Mission
- Visitation
- Worship
- Leadership
- Groupings
- Decision making

These relational characteristics draw people to worship, provide them with a sense of mission for their own lives, and give them help, hope, home, and satisfaction. The more compelling the relational factors, the more willing people are to put up with occasionally inadequate parking and an uncomfortably crowded sanctuary on special Sundays. People will also put up with inadequate facilities and parking on regular Sundays when the relational factors are compelling. (See *Dynamic Worship* for a number of suggestions about seating capacity.) Congregations who are carrying out a compelling long-range mission plan that includes shepherding, worship, groupings, leadership, and staffing objectives find that people will tolerate crowded facilities more frequently during the year.

Thus develop the following:

- The strength and outreach of a compelling, compassionate mission
- The congregation's and staff's caring and the quality of their shepherding

- Worship services that are corporate and dynamic; preaching that is helpful and hopeful; music that is stirring and inspiring; strong choirs at each major service
- Established, healthy groupings and new groupings started on a regular basis
- The continuity of competent, compassionate leaders, pastor, and staff

As you plan the number of major worship services for each week and the related schedule of church school and meetings of other significant relational groupings, consider

- the persons, families, groupings you would like to reach and serve,
- the most convenient times for them, and
- the strength of the worship services, church school, and groupings you plan to develop.

The more options you offer, the more people you will reach. The more convenient the options, the more new people you will reach. The stronger the options, the more frequently everyone will participate.

Two church schools on Sunday are less expensive than one, provided the congregation invests in the additional competent, part-time or full-time staff to develop the second. It is not appropriate to ask a current staff member to do double duty. Each major church school deserves its own competent professional.

Having only one church school on Sunday increases the number of classrooms needing to be built by 50 percent to 60 percent, sometimes higher. That is a very expensive way to proceed. Two church schools use the rooms more fully, save considerable building expense, and provide better, more spacious rooms.

Congregations are increasingly offering church school during the week as well as on Sunday. Adequate professional staff is central to this effort. The sessions are usually scheduled for after school or weekday evenings or Saturday mornings and are mostly for preschool and elementary-age children and their parents. Sometimes the parents' educational grouping is scheduled at another time during the week near where they work. Then these families worship together on Sunday.

Look at your facilities with rigor. Maximize their use in every possible way. You may decide to use some of your space in new ways. Many of the old ways may no longer suit your current mission.

Years ago some churches built a room specifically for the committee meetings of the church. Times have changed. We have fewer committees meeting inside the church and more mission teams serving in the community. That room may now be used for the weekday preschool program and as part of the nursery in the evenings and on the weekends.

Years ago some congregations built full commercial kitchens to cook everything from scratch. Several times a year volunteers prepared large meals to serve the congregation and the community. Times have changed. The mission has grown. Some congregations decide to dispense with the commercial kitchen, or use it in a different way, and to have more of a covered-dish, microwave kitchen.

Years ago some congregations built church parlors, which were rarely used, and then only by a few people. Times have changed. The mission has grown. Now that space is used by Bible study groups, prayer groups, adult Sunday school classes, bridal parties, and for conferences and workshops.

Before you build new space, discover as many creative ways as possible to use your present space. Look closely at whether earlier uses of the space now no longer serve the mission. Consider first what current space you can improve, and only afterward what facilities need to be added.

A CONGREGATIONAL RESPONSE
TO THE CROSS

Service is stronger than survival.
> *We are the People of Service.*

Sacrifice is stronger than striving.
> *We are the People of Sacrifice.*

Giving is stronger than getting.
> *We are the Giving People.*

The cross of Calvary is stronger than the empires of the world.
> *We are the People of the Cross.*

The crucified Christ is stronger than the powers of this world.
> *We are the People of the Crucified Christ.*
> *We are the Calvary People.*
> *We are the People of Sacrifice.*

7:

The Key to an Extraordinary First Year

Let everything that breathes praise the lord.
Ps. 150:6

In an age of mission, two things are true:

- It only works in baseball.
- The right mission plan and building program will give you a five-year window of opportunity and momentum.

I was working as a consultant with a congregation. They were building a new sanctuary to replace an older one. We were meeting with the architects, studying the plans for the new sanctuary.

Halfway through the meeting the realization came to me that it only works in the movies, it only works in Iowa, and it only works in baseball, when the voice said,

"Build it and they will come."

It doesn't work in most of the planet, and it doesn't work in churches in our time.

I said to the group, "We've been planning to build a new sanctuary the same size as the old one. What we know is that during the last twenty years the worship attendance had declined to twenty percent of the sanctuary's capacity.

"We've been assuming that the new sanctuary, because of its newness and attractiveness, will draw people. But the attendance at worship was down to almost nothing. We'll be lucky in the new sanctuary to do just a little better than we are now doing.

"The old sanctuary, as attractive as it was, was not filling itself. The new sanctuary, as beautiful as it will be, will not fill itself.

"Let's first discover the mission to which God is inviting us and then decide, based on the size of our mission, the size of sanctuary that will serve the mission."

Over time, with much prayer and thought, we developed a mission to serve the children and their families in three nearby elementary schools. The components of the mission plan include an after-school program, music instruction, summer recreation, and family enrichment programs. The congregation directs its enthusiasm toward the mission; the building of the sanctuary took its rightful subordinate place.

The principle I have come to is "Mission, then mortar." This is really the first of three helpful principles:

• Mission, then mortar
• Build to grow
• Grow, then build

In my earliest days, the principle I encouraged was, Grow, then build. Thus we would wait until we were overflowing with people, and then we would build new facilities to relieve the terribly crowded conditions. The difficulty was that by the time we moved in, we had outgrown the new facilities.

"Grow, then build" is still helpful. I use this principle with some caution. Sometimes we are too crowded the day we move in. Sometimes we wait too long to build and thereby lose the moment.

With more experience, I discovered the principle "Build to grow." It is possible to build new facilities to create growth. This was especially true in a time when churchgoing was a part of social conformity. The principle still works under some conditions in our time; still, it is best used with caution. Congregations who build buildings without building mission simply don't grow. They end up with too much debt and too much unused space. The new building alone will not bring growth.

A house doesn't make a home; people do. A building doesn't make a church; mission does. Mission gives heart and soul to mortar. All three principles work, and the one that works best is, Mission, then mortar.

A FIVE-YEAR WINDOW

Congregations usually grow their mission in quantum leaps, not gradually. When you have both a mission action plan and a creative, constructive building program, the combined result creates a five-year window of momentum and opportunity.

Make good use of the first year; then you will gain all five years of momentum and opportunity for mission and service. Should you throw away that first year, you throw away all five years. Develop your mission action plan with as much specific detail as the blueprint for your building.

Many churches become preoccupied with the doors, walls, and windows—the details in the blueprint for the building. They fail to develop an equally specific and concrete blueprint for their mission. Their focus is too easily diverted to the building.

A blueprint for mission needs to be specific in naming objectives, content, staffing, and dates. Don't be caught empty-handed when the construction is completed. What would happen if a newly built grocery store held the grand opening for its building but then took six months to get the produce section staffed and supplied, ten months to get the frozen food section in, and fifteen months to get the full staff in place?

Too many churches finish constructing their building and then take six to fifteen months after moving in to figure out their community outreach, their mission service program, their staffing, and their congregational development program.

Put as much energy, prayer, and wisdom into developing your detailed mission plan as you do your building plan. You can have your most competent leaders serve on a leadership team that concentrates first on your specific mission plan, then on the building plan. Or you can have one group of your most competent leaders serve on the mission blueprint team and another group serve on the building blueprint team, which reports to the mission blueprint team. Do not do it the other way around. The mission drives the building.

SET THE DATE

Planning for your move into the new building is like planning for a wedding. First you set the date for the wedding. People who set a date for their wedding tend to get married. People who never set a date for the wedding hardly ever get married. So your first step is to set the date for your move into the new building. Think about the year, month, and week you plan to move in.

Once you have selected the specific date, plan the construction schedule backward from that date. In planning a wedding, people decide when it will be, then they figure out when the rehearsal will be, when the clothes for the wedding need to be finished and how far ahead of that they need to be ordered, when the wedding invitations need to be sent out, and so on.

Don't count forward from the date of the groundbreaking or from the date you choose an architect. The project will drag. Time will be lost. Momentum will wither. Uncertainty will creep in. And you may end up moving in at a poor time of year.

The best two times of year to move into new facilities in the Northern Hemisphere are September/October or January/February. November or December is too busy a time. If you move in during September/October, you can build momentum toward the first Christmas. If you move in during January/February, you can build momentum toward the first Easter. It's not advisable to move in April or May. Some will propose the romantic notion of moving in on Easter. If you do that, you'll have that one glorious Sunday, then you'll move quickly to the summer slump. The art is to move in well before the summer slump so that you build enough energy to see you through the first summer.

If you move into new facilities just before a predictable summer slowdown, people will begin to ask why you made all of those improvements, or built so big a building, and why you have acquired so much debt. People may begin to see the new building as a drag rather than an advance. When that perception begins to take hold, it becomes very difficult to shake. People's giving to their building pledges begins to drag and becomes reluctant. The original critics of the building program resurface and complain even more loudly. A troubling time ensues. All because of moving in at the wrong time of year.

Set a reasonable date for moving in; then plan the construction schedule backward from that date. Although sometimes the date for moving in will get postponed because bad weather delayed construction, your architect and your contractor are responsible for bringing the project in on time. They are your employees. They work for you; you do not work for them. They also have an obligation to keep within the budget. Sometimes a project will come in 10 or 15 percent over budget. All the more reason for it to come in on time. And if the construction is delayed, all the more reason for it to come in within budget. The best building projects come in on time and within budget.

MISSION-BUILDING SCHEDULE

Once you have the date to move in, create a mission-building schedule that works to that date. Think through the objectives and the deadlines to be achieved during the two years prior to moving in, one year prior, and six months prior. Set objectives and dates for the first three months and the first year in the new facility.

Table 7.1 is an example of a mission building schedule. From one church to the next—and from one project to the next—the sequence, the time frames, and the dates for objectives will vary. The point of the example is to show you how to create a specific set of steps with reasonable time horizons to achieve your move-in date and your best first year.

The art is to create a realistic countdown schedule that effectively launches the first year of your mission and building.

Your First Year

Let the first year in your new facilities be a full year of celebration. Don't celebrate for just one Sunday—that throws away the whole first year. Have the fun of a year of celebration. During this first year, share eight to ten major events that serve as your gifts to the community and that help the entire community to discover the mission, resources, and compassion of your congregation in fresh ways.

Table 7.1 Our Mission Building Schedule

Objective	Date
1. Our celebration year	full year
2. Community mission and outreach	first three months
3. Our first Sunday	specific date
4. Community mission and outreach	three months prior
5. Leadership development	four to six months prior
6. Blueprint for mission for first year	six months prior
7. Groundbreaking	twelve months prior
8. Building fund celebration	fourteen months prior
9. Mission planning team for first year	fifteen months prior
10. Building fund campaign	seventeen months prior
11. Completed bids	nineteen months prior
12. Working drawings	twenty-one months prior
13. Preliminary drawings	twenty-four months prior
14. Selection of architect	twenty-seven months prior
15. Selection of building committee	thirty months prior
16. Long-range mission action plan	thirty-two months prior

In both *Dynamic Worship* and *Effective Church Finances* you will find discussions of Major Community Sundays. This material will help you greatly in developing a year of celebration.

Your First Sunday

The first Sunday celebration and consecration is threefold: of our mission, that we will share God's mission well in the community and beyond; of ourselves, to live well together

as family; of our facilities, to serve the mission. The consecration is a dedication of people as well as place.

Invite the whole community. Encourage your families
to invite their friends, their co-workers, their extended family. It will be like a wedding feast, a great banquet, a memo-
rable and holy time. There will be festive music—adult and
children's choirs, instrumental groups—to help us celebrate.
There will be a time of prayer and sharing, singing and
Scripture. The pastor and several people in the congregation will share their hopes and compassion. There will be a
time for fellowship and festive refreshments.

Community Mission and Outreach

Develop two significant stages of community mission and
outreach. The first stage is the three months prior to moving
in. Let this three months be the best effort your congregation has ever made to reach people in the community. Advance some components of the mission before you move in.

The second stage is during the first three months in
your new facilities. As the saying goes, you can never make
a first impression the second time. You will never have these
first three months again. They are one of the best opportunities to expand the strength of your mission in the community. Use them well.

In *Visiting in an Age of Mission* you will find many helpful suggestions about ways to reach and serve people in the
community during this decisive time.

Leadership Development

Knowing the specifics of your first-year plan at least six
months before moving in, you can do excellent volunteer re-
cruitment and leadership development in the sixth, fifth,

and fourth months before moving in. Do your leadership re-
cruitment in the community as well as in the church. You'll
discover that when you have a compelling mission plan,
people in the community will want to come on board and
become part of the mission teams.

By doing the recruiting and leadership training in the
sixth, fifth, and fourth months before moving in, you'll be
giving people ample lead time to look forward to the volunteer work they will have the fun of participating in as you
move.

Last-minute recruiting causes unnecessary stress for
volunteers and leaders. They don't get to enjoy the genuine fun and pleasure of the celebration. They do not have
the time to train themselves more fully, nor do they have
the time to think through the creative, new ways they can
share their best gifts as volunteers. Recruiting well in advance gives volunteers the chance to be at their creative best
as you move in.

Blueprint for Mission

Have well in place six months prior to moving in the detailed plan for the first year. This includes the specific objectives for mission, shepherding, worship, groupings, staffing,
and major community events.

Earlier you created your long-range mission action
plan. That plan looks three to five years ahead (in some areas, five to seven years or longer). Based on that long-range
plan, you develop a specific plan for the first year of mission
in the improved and/or new space. In order to achieve this
detailed, first-year plan, your "Year of Celebration" team
will begin working on the specifics approximately twelve to
fifteen months before the move. This gives them, in fact, six
to nine months to create the plan so that it has been com-
pletely developed six months prior to moving in.

Groundbreaking

This a time of celebration and consecration of our mission, ourselves, and our facilities. The reasonable time for breaking ground depends on how long it takes to build what we plan to build. Sometimes we break ground fifteen to eighteen months before the planned move-in date. Should you be making significant improvements on an existing building, I encourage you to have a groundbreaking to celebrate the beginning of these improvements as well.

Building Fund Celebration

Sometimes we break ground soon after launching the building fund campaign, when we are confident of the funding. Other times we raise the building fund pledges and then wait six to twelve months in order to have some of the giving fund in hand before we break ground.

Three-year building fund pledges are typically given based on visible progress. The sooner the mission moves forward and the construction is under way, the sooner the giving increases. If you wait a year to begin, you will not have received one-third of the pledges. Yes, you will have received some gifts, but the giving happens in relation to visible progress in the mission and the building.

Building Fund Campaign

An excellent building campaign can be accomplished, start to finish, in three months or less. The campaign focuses on the blueprint for mission as well as the blueprint for the building. Teach the mission; you will raise more money. People will give to people—to the mission—as well as to the building.

Completed Bids

People pledge more generously and confidently when bids are in and they know how much it is really going to cost. If the building fund campaign precedes the completed bids, you'll have more difficulty raising the money. It works in that sequence only when we are already reasonably sure of the real cost. Otherwise we run the risk of discovering that the actual costs are going to be higher than we targeted in the pledge drive; then we are not able to build all the facilities we had planned and raised pledges for. An awkward position.

Preliminary Drawings

When the preliminary drawings are complete, I strongly encourage you to have one to three excellent contractors study them thoroughly. Gain their wisdom and experience on how to streamline the plans and build the facility simply and within budget.

Don't wait until the working drawings have been finished to have your first consultation with a contractor—you'd find yourself reducing the plan and having to redo the working drawings, and this would cost you time, money, and momentum. It is both discouraging and unfair to go back to the congregation and say, "We have to reduce the plan or raise more money."

The key is to get one or more contractors to examine the preliminary drawings. Their wisdom and realism at this stage will help greatly. Architects usually do a reasonable job of estimating the costs of a building. But the contractor has the primary stake in being able to tell accurately what it will actually cost. Contractors, not architects, make their profit—or lose money—based on the accuracy of their estimates.

It's unfair to subject a congregation to a series of bad-news announcements about cost overruns. Regrettably, the contractor is sometimes allowed to be the fall guy for the bad news, usually when the project is far along. It's far more helpful to gain the wisdom of a contractor at the preliminary-drawing stage.

Choosing an Architect

The process for selecting an architect and the criteria to use are discussed in chapter 9. For the moment it is important to note that this selection occurs after the congregation has developed its long-range mission action plan.

When you're working with an architect who is familiar with this book, and with the Twelve Keys principles and planning process, you can include that person at an earlier stage. These days many architects are using the Twelve Keys principles in their work with congregations. But if your architect is not familiar with the Twelve Keys, bringing him or her on board too early may tend to lead your project away from building the mission first, and, as a result, constructing the building may become the mission.

Choosing a Building Committee

This will be discussed in depth in chapter 8. At this point it is important to observe that the congregation as a whole participates in developing its future mission action plan. Frequently a Twelve Keys consultant assists the congregation in developing this plan.

Sometimes a building committee and a Twelve Keys consultant together lead the congregation in determining its long-range mission plan. When this occurs, it is crucial that the building committee see itself as a mission-building committee, genuinely searching for the mission to which God is leading the congregation. The building committee has a mission focus first.

With the move-in date set and the mission-building schedule in place, you will have an extraordinary first year. It will be great not because of the new space. It will be an extraordinary year because

- you have developed a compelling long-range mission action plan,
- you have a creative, detailed plan for your Year of Celebration, and
- you are moving into excellent facilities.

A PRAYER FOR HELPFUL MISSION

Lord God, help us to fall in love with people.
Help us to not wait on people to fall in love with us.

Lord God, help us to build on our strengths in healthy,
  prayerful ways.
Help us to not be preoccupied with problems, weaknesses,
  size.

Lord God, help us to discover new ways with creativity and
  flexibility.
Help us to not continue practices that no longer work.

Lord God, help us to serve persons in healthful ways in
  Christ.
Help us to not develop dependent—codependent relations.

Lord God, help us to live with a confident sense of hope in
  God's grace.
Help us to not be preoccupied with status, standing,
  survival.

Grant us a rich, full life in mission.

       In the name of Christ, amen.

8:

Creating an Effective Building Team

For just as the body is one and has many
members, and all the members of the body,
though many, are one body, so it is with Christ.
1 Cor. 12:12

LEADERS

Excellent leaders create excellent facilities. In growing your mission, improving present space, and building new facilities, draw together the leaders to serve as your building team using these criteria:

- Look at the whole, not the parts.
- Have a love and yearning for mission.
- Look long range, not short term.
- Have the reciprocal trust and respect of the congregation and the community.
- Bring wisdom, judgment, vision, and common sense to the team.

- Be people of prayer and compassion.
- Work well together as a team.

These criteria will help you discover who will serve best on your building team, or, if you prefer, building committee.

THE BUILDING TEAM

Building teams usually get organized in one of three ways:

1. A building team, with congregational task force groups related to the core team

2. A small building committee that oversees a modest project

3. Individual committees for each component, with coordinating sessions for the committee chairs

Using the first model, you build a stronger mission and better facilities in less time, with less money, have more fun, with more volunteers, raise more money, and serve more people in mission.

The second way works with a modest project that already has strong grassroots congregational involvement. But on a medium-size or large-scale project, this approach creates a serious problem of ownership—the small building committee has ownership of the project, but the congregation does not. Further, the project does not benefit from the excellent ideas present in the congregation.

The third way is cumbersome and requires too much coordination. It takes too long and usually results in lost momentum. Its focus is on the parts more than the whole.

With the first method, the focus is on the whole. You gain the leadership of a core building team that in turn involves many persons in the congregation in task forces. The core team provides a clear sense of direction and unity to the whole. The project usually progresses on schedule and within budget.

Most important, the group behaves as a team. They focus on the whole and work well together, as a unit. They pool their best wisdom and energy. It's not a collection of competing interests, nor do the team members behave like a loosely connected gathering of individuals functioning as a committee.

The building team's marching orders are the congregation's mission action plan. Members of your building committee have been involved in helping to create your plan, and they count on the facilities to live out the mission objectives of the plan.

They don't start over. They don't create an alternative future. They don't become preoccupied with the new building. They are faithful to your congregation's mission action plan.

Some building teams benefit from consultation with an experienced long-range planning consultant. In fact, the consultant may already have been working with the congregation, pastor, and staff on developing their mission action plan, a consequence of which is the creation of a building committee.

The planning consultant continues to work with your congregation through and beyond the building project, helping to focus on the whole of your long-range plan. It is not that your consultant leaves and an architect comes in. We are doing more than building a building.

The building team, pastor, staff, planning consultant, architect, and contractor function together as a team. This team offers leadership for the task forces in the congregation who develop excellent ideas and good suggestions for specific areas of the project.

Increasingly, competent architects are training themselves in the Twelve Keys principles. While their primary focus is appropriately on the building project, they contribute knowledgeably to developing the whole of the mission toward which churches are headed.

BUILDING TEAM PROGRESS

Early in the building committee's work together, it is important for the team to organize how it plans to work together. Your building committee will make excellent progress when, in the beginning, you help each person on the team create a description of what each plans to contribute to the team. This leadership description includes

- two to four key action objectives related to the project that each team member plans to achieve in the coming one to three years
- the major responsibilities vital to achieving these objectives
- authority in decision making, leadership, and budget decisions
- straight-line accountability to the team
- one to two specific competencies each member plans to cultivate
- the prayer resources that will undergird each person and the team as a whole

The team has its focus on the whole, and each person achieves certain objectives and has certain responsibilities on behalf of the team.

TASK FORCES

Each task force will be guided by your long-range plan, including the key objectives for mission, shepherding, worship, groupings, leadership, and staffing. Then each task force pools its best wisdom for its distinctive area of concentration. The nature and number of task forces will vary from one church to the next and from one building project to the next.

A task force develops a realistic, achievable set of objectives for facility needs. Its job is not to develop a shopping list of wants and wishes—that only necessitates extra work for the building committee, which would have to sift through and separate needs from wishes. The task force has the capacity to separate basic facility needs from their own dreams. Yes, the group will do some visioning and dreaming. Then it will take the important step of deciding what will be genuinely helpful to the mission.

The task force does not behave like a group of children turned loose in a candy store. It develops a responsible, reasonable set of suggestions for its area of work.

Just as the building committee does not reinvent the church's long-range plan, neither do the task forces. The mission action plan is developed first, precisely to guide the building team and task forces in their work with facilities.

Depending on the specific building project, many congregations have found some of these types of task forces helpful:

- parking, landscaping, exterior lighting, signage
- worship, sanctuary, chapel
- music groupings
- lighting, acoustics, sound
- interior design
- fellowship, recreation, community life center
- food service
- families with children
- families with youth
- single adult ministries
- adult ministries
- senior adults ministries
- administration and volunteers' work areas

Task forces consist of eight to fifteen people, sometimes twenty. Those in the group bring wisdom, distinctive competencies, and experience suited to the specific focus of the group. They network with many people in the congregation and the community to gather the best suggestions possible. They are the grassroots link to both the congregation and the community.

A task force works for a short time in a highly intensive way. Then it is on call to the building team for any further assistance it might render. A task force does not usually meet weekly or monthly over a two- or three-year period. It functions as a streamlined, short-term team, and it discovers the best suggestions for its distinctive area.

CONGREGATIONAL PLANNING

Frequently the building committee sponsors a congregational planning event to gather the best ideas of a wide range of people. The art is to encourage the involvement of as many people in the congregation as would like to participate.

People are encouraged to select the group with which they want to share and have fun. The groups are convened by the distinctive task forces. Everyone—entire families, children, and youth—are encouraged to participate. Usually they participate in discussion in groups of ten to fifteen persons.

The spirit is to count on excellent ideas and suggestions. We have this one chance to build well for our mission, our families, and our future. Few people, in their whole lifetime, have the opportunity to share in such a remarkable privilege and adventure.

God has blessed us. Be in prayer. Be as creative and wise as possible when you gather for this congregational planning event. Take pictures of each planning group. Invite each person to sign the historical register. Have someone write a brief narrative of what happened. We are creating the future and history at the same time.

Help the sessions to be ones of good fun and good times, deep thought and solid creativity. Help people to discover one another as family and friends in richer, fuller ways. Help them to sense the moving, stirring presence of God in their midst, leading them forward with compassion and vision.

LOOKING TO THE LONG TERM

As you contemplate building any new facility, look to the future of your mission. Match the size of the building to the size of the mission. The larger the mission, the larger the building.

Too many congregations underbuild. They focus on the size and cost of the building and lose track of the size of the mission. They focus on the initial cost and not on the long-term mission for years to come—helping persons with their lives and destinies in the name of Christ.

With major buildings, we have the chance to do this once in a lifetime. For most of us, God gives us this one possibility of matching mission and facilities. We need to do it well.

When you think of your new sanctuary, for instance, look toward the coming hundred years. See the people across the years who will discover Christ there. Look toward those whose lives will be enriched, whose families will be strengthened, whose futures will be restored. Think of the marriages that will begin there, the people who will be baptized there, the friends who will discover one another there, the rites of parting that will be shared there. Consider the persons who will worship God deeply and fully there.

Look forward to the spirit of compassion and sense of community that will be experienced there. Look forward to the new insights and wisdom that will be discovered there.

Look forward to the celebrations of God's grace that will happen there.

Think of the decisions made there that will shape people's lives and destinies, strengthen the quality of life in the community, and advance the mission across the planet. Think of the prayers that will be lifted there. Build well the mission and the mortar.

SHEPHERDING THE TRANSITION

A building project provides a key time to enhance the shepherding that is offered in the church. If you develop a solid shepherding team, people stay with you through the trials and tribulations of a building project.

People finally do not make the transition because of logic, urgent need, or reasonable cost. They move forward because of the compassion, assurance, and care of a shepherding team, the pastor, and several key shepherds.

With any building project there will be anticipation and anxiety. The reassurance of a shepherd helps people through this.

No matter how much we try to limit them, the number of meetings and the number of decisions increases. Sometimes, in the midst of those decisions, things are said that are later regretted. The reconciliation skills of a shepherd help people through this.

Building projects harbor surprises and require revisions. Some are happy surprises; some are difficult and troubling. The steady hand of a shepherd helps people through this.

With a building project, everyone—the building team, the task forces, and the congregation as a whole—invests more time and energy. Sometimes we feel stretched thin. The encouraging word of a shepherd helps people through this.

One mistake pastors sometimes make during a building project is to become involved almost as a second architect or contractor. When this happens, they neglect their role as shepherd. The same is true with some of the congregation's gifted, shepherding leaders. They become caught up in the details of working drawings for the building and leave their shepherding less well tended.

It is precisely during a building project that the shepherding of the pastor and gifted leaders is crucial. When you embark on a building project, pay particular attention to the congregation's needs for care.

Our intentional shepherding focuses on the everyday life of people, their ordinary times, their special times of celebration, and the tough, tragic times. We offer our care with a deeper quality and a fuller range and include especially the people on the building team and the task forces—not in terms of their role in the building plan but in relation to their lives. Sometimes in the bustling activities of a building project, these persons and their families are overlooked when it comes to solid shepherding. We think, "We see them in the meetings; if they need help, they'll say so."

We shepherd in relation to the building project itself. We don't wait for the anxiety levels to rise or until after key decisions have been made. We shepherd in advance; our care is proactive. The less shepherding, the more bickering. The more shepherding, the less bickering. And even here our shepherding is not finally primarily related to the events of the building project. It is predominately focused on the events taking place in people's lives.

Shepherding is not holding people's hands through the building project. People's lives go on during the project. As all-consuming as a building project sometimes is, it is not the only thing happening. We tend to lose our perspective on who we are and whose we are when we allow a building project to overwhelm us. What helps us keep our perspective is the skillful shepherding of a pastor and several gifted shepherding leaders.

With excellent leaders, a solid building team, congregational task forces, and a substantial shepherding team, the building project will move forward in strength.

9:

Selecting Your Architect

Therefore, since we are surrounded by so great a cloud of witnesses, let us also lay aside every weight and sin which clings so closely, and let us run with perseverance the race that is set before us, looking to Jesus. *Heb. 12:1–2*

Among the most important decisions the building team will make is the selection of an architect. This person is not the leader of the team—this is not an architect-driven project, it is a mission-driven project. The building committee and its chair serve as the key leaders of the project. At the same time, the architect is one of their major resources and plays a pivotal role in the project.

In order to help you evaluate and choose from among a number of architects, Table 9.1 is provided for your use. Never select your architect on the basis of design alone. There is more to constructing a building than just design. Select the person you will work well with on the basis of all ten of these criteria.

Table 9.1 Criteria for Architectural Study Process Worksheet for Evaluation

	Rating Value	A	Firm B	C
1. Creativity and excellence of design matches congregation's mission	10			
2. Integrity of projects, structural, functional, long term	10			
3. Estimate-to-bid accuracy in recent projects of comparable nature	10			
4. Execution of design (construction matches design)	10			
5. Ability to meet timelines demonstrated in recent projects	10			
6. Team ability—with building committee, its various task forces, pastor, staff, planning consultant	10			
7. Ability to work with contractor, consulting firms, subcontractors	10			
8. Ability to use the firm's best people on the project during coming three years	10			
9. Ability to work with the building committee's project inspector	10			
10. Reasonable structure and schedule of payments	10			

CREATIVITY

Does the creativity of the design suit the specific mission of your congregation? Does the architect have a compelling compassion for your congregation's mission? Has that person had recent experience in designing excellent facilities for such a mission?

The design should not be the ambition of the architect. We don't want a monument to the architect's design abilities. We're ultimately looking for a design that lives out the sense of home and family that is important to your congregation's mission. The most creative architects have the ability to match the building to the congregation rather than trying to mold the congregation to fit some spectacular building.

Your distinctive mission may be with children and their families, so you would want the design to be child friendly. If you're a family congregation, you would build a family sanctuary, not a cathedral sanctuary.

Evaluate the architect's recent projects. Was the design fully developed prior to construction? When a design has not been fully thought through, more changes occur during construction, and costs increase. Some building committees have had to go back to the congregation for a "Second Mile" campaign to raise additional funds to cover such costs. The better the design, the fewer the changes.

INTEGRITY OF CONSTRUCTION

Look at the structural, functional, and long-term integrity of the architect's recent projects. When you consider the structural intregity of previous projects, ask yourself whether the buildings are genuinely well built and have lasting value. In the best-built church buildings, the roof doesn't leak and the rafters don't sag.

Functional integrity means the buildings work for the people who use them. In previous projects, are the intended functions of the buildings carried out easily on a daily basis?

After people move into a building, they sometimes discover that some element of the design hinders what they are trying to do in mission, worship, and scheduling. Certain rooms intended to work well in a church's mission don't always. For example, rooms for preschool and elementary-age children. The congregation finds that the functionality they hoped for does not really exist.

You also want an architect who understands that many of the people coming to worship will arrive within fifteen minutes of one another. That is, many people show up all at once and many people leave all at once. And when one service follows another, some people are coming to 11:00 A.M. worship, while others who were at 9:30 A.M. church school or worship have not yet left. The design of the building and its relation to adjacent parking areas can help this flow well or can impede the process.

Consider also whether the buildings have long-term integrity. Study previous projects to see whether they have a reasonable life span with minimal preventative maintenance, ongoing restoration, and major emergency repairs.

Sometimes a congregation is led to construct a building that is inexpensive on the front end and very expensive to maintain in the long term. You will not be well served by an architect who leads you in that direction—and you will end up with buildings that do not serve the mission.

Such buildings force the congregation to commit too much of its annual budget to contingency maintenance and to have too many capital fund drives over the years to fix up the buildings. And these efforts drain away the energy and money that could go to mission.

ACCURACY OF PROJECTED COSTS

Consider whether the architect's estimates of costs have been reasonably accurate in relation to contractor bids and actual construction costs in recent projects. Look at the extent to which specific contractors and leaders of similar projects have evidenced their satisfaction with the estimate-to-bid accuracy of the architect.

Many architects have a reliable rate of accuracy, and their cost estimates come very close to actual costs. Being off by 5 to 15 percent is perhaps understandable—we usually build into the estimate some contingency amount in that range. But for an architect to be off 20 to 45 percent indicates that you cannot trust his or her cost estimates.

EXECUTION OF DESIGN

Study whether the execution of previous designs is successfully achieved in the construction of the facilities. Recent projects will have demonstrated whether this is the case or not. There may have been omissions, midcourse changes, or additions that altered the original design. Consider how significantly these have altered the actual outcome.

Don't select your architect on the basis of that person's sincerity. You're not looking for the person who seems the most committed and dedicated. Sincerity will not bring the building in on time or keep it from costing more than makes sense; nor will it keep the roof from leaking. Make your decision on the basis of whether there is competent execution in recent projects.

TIMELINES

Look at demonstrated ability to meet the deadlines at each stage of a building project. When you set your date for moving in—and develop the construction timelines backward from that date—will you be able to count on the architect to deliver on time?

If the final preliminary drawings were delayed, working drawings were not completed on time, or the specifications for construction lagged behind, this may teach you that the person you're considering has developed a habitual pattern of being late with their own work.

Fortunately, there are many competent architects who have demonstrated their ability to both do their own work on time and to bring a whole project in on time. When a project is completed on time, these are some of the results that are achieved:

- We start strong in the new facilities, serving persons in a fuller, more helpful mission.
- The morale and motivation of the congregation is high.
- The expectancy of the community is strong.
- The year of celebration is done well.
- The giving of the congregation continues on pace.
- The possibility of new giving to the mission and the building increases.

When a building project is delayed, however, these are some of the results:

- We start poorly and lose that much time in helping the people we wish to serve through the building project.
- The morale and motivation of the congregation becomes disjointed and low.
- The expectancy of the community is lost; the community moves on to other things.
- The year of celebration is delayed; we are at risk of losing the five-year window of opportunity.
- The giving of the congregation waits on the building to move forward.

- The possibility of new giving to the mission and the building is delayed; some giving is lost.

Timelines are decisive to the mission.

TEAM ABILITY

Is there reasonable evidence that the architect will work well as part of your building committee, its various task forces, your pastor, your staff, and your long-range planning consultant?

You are looking for the architect who will share his or her best wisdom, experience, common sense, and judgment and who will coach the rest of the team as they seek to understand architecture. We're not looking for a passive, placid people-pleaser or a domineering, dictatorial prima donna.

You do not want an architect who panders excessively to the building committee and the pastor. Being pleasing and placating is not team ability. Nor do you want, on the other extreme, an architect who does not listen, who obstinately insists on his own way, and who has a dictatorial attitude.

You do want a confident, strong-minded architect who will share his or her views assertively and positively. Otherwise you won't get the best wisdom and judgment for your money. You do want an architect who is compatible with the building team.

One clue to an architect's team ability is to see how he or she behaves with co-workers in the architectural firm. Ask yourself how well this firm functions as a team. Invite comments in this regard from leaders and pastors who have worked with the architect on recent projects.

Your project will be best achieved when you work together as a team in a genuinely collaborative, cooperative way. By pooling their wisdom and creativity, members of the team discover the best way forward.

CONSTRUCTION ABILITY

Look at the architect's compatibility and capacity to work with various consulting firms, contractors, and subcontractors.

In the past has the architect consulted with the very best resources, both firms and individuals? Look at the person's recent experience in working with the most competent landscapers, interior designers, sound experts, lighting experts, and so on in your area.

It is not simply a question of whether the architect has a group of various resource firms and people. Over time most architects develop a network of such firms with whom they habitually work. The key is whether they are working with some of the very best in your area. The best resource firms tend to work with the best architects. They tend not to work with mediocre architects.

Thus you learn a lot about an architect's competencies by looking at the resources with whom he or she works. And it is most important that the architect has demonstrated the ability to work well with this range of consultants. Invite comments from firms with whom he or she has worked on recent projects.

Consider whether, and to what extent, the architect has demonstrated the ability to work well with the specific contractor you plan to use and, depending on the nature and extent of the project, with any of the subcontractors that will be involved. It is much likelier that a project will progress on time and within budget, and will be well built, when the architect and the contractor have a constructive, cooperative relationship.

USING THE BEST PEOPLE

Can the architectural firm focus the attention of their best people on the project during the coming three to four years—that is, during design, construction, and the first full year in the new facility? When you hire an architectural firm, you must have a clear contractual understanding as to which specific person or persons within the firm will have this project as their priority.

Look most closely at the competencies and credentials of the specific project architect the firm will assign you. While it is true that we hire the whole firm and have the benefit of a whole firm's expertise, it finally comes down to the day-to-day work of the project architect.

It is usually to your advantage to have as your project architect a principal of the firm with considerable experience. When a person of this quality is the project architect four things happen:

1. We receive the day-to-day, seasoned work of an important architect.

2. The day-to-day involvement of the principal commands the best attention of the whole firm.

3. The project usually runs on schedule.

4. The project usually stays within budget.

SUPERVISION

Evaluate the supervisory capacity of the architect in two ways. First, look at the way in which he or she has related to previous building projects on a regular basis during construction. This has to do with both reasonable availability and attention to details as the project is under way. Second, evaluate whether the architect will work well with whomever the building committee selects to be its day-to-day representative as project inspector during the course of construction.

You will need to agree on the one person from your team who will directly interface with the architect and contractor during construction. This may be a volunteer, yet more often this person is employed by the congregation as project inspector on behalf of the building committee. This person has a solid background in construction, knows building specifications thoroughly, and has an excellent eye for quality control.

Individuals on the building committee do not directly relate to either the architect or the contractor. They relate to them only through the committee as a whole. You need to avoid having one member of the building committee tell a contractor one thing and another member something else.

The interface during construction is between the architect, contractor, and the church's project inspector. Look for the architect who will have a constructive relationship with the project inspector.

FEE STRUCTURE

Look at whether the architectural firm and the building committee can agree on a reasonable fee structure. Further, look at equitable timing for both the architectural work and the schedule of payments when it is done.

Don't make your selection solely on the basis of the fee. There is more to it than simply getting a bargain price. A bargain has a way of costing you dearly in the long run.

Create an appropriate relationship of deadlines and payment schedule. When the work deadlines are met, funds are released as payment, based on the completion of work. When the deadlines are not met, no funds are released for payment until the work is completed.

Some fee structures include merit pay for work done ahead of time and penalty fees for delayed work. You can decide whether such incentives are appropriate to your project. The key is to create a reasonable fee structure, work schedule, and payment schedule that is fair to the parties involved.

OTHER CONSIDERATIONS

When you reach a tentative conclusion and have narrowed down the field of primary architectural firms you are considering, spot-check the references of each firm under consideration for

- the quality of the work
- the timeliness of the work
- how closely they adhered to budget
- how recently the work was done

Look at the consulting firms they propose to use as well. Secure the exact budget figures each architectural firm is allocating for consulting firm resources. Be certain it is adequate. Be cautious if a firm mentions a figure for landscaping consultation that would permit only a minimal plan.

The best architectural proposals confirm the dollar amount they are budgeting for each consulting firm and how many days and/or how much project consultation that is purchasing. Ensure that you will benefit from the best consulting resources. A minimal budget by the architectural firm will not help.

Look for a project architect and architectural firm who are respected for their character, integrity, and honesty. Given a choice, choose the competent architect with excellent character and a solid professional reputation over the less competent architect (even if they have done lots of church buildings).

You want the architect who has a solid sense of self-esteem, whose word is his bond, and who will deal with you in an honest, fair-minded way. Finally, when you make your selection, you lend the name of your church to the firm you select. You endorse it as a worthwhile, excellent firm. Select the competent firm that brings solid character to the project, whether or not it has done a church before.

Considering a joint venture with two architectural firms? We are looking for the best resources available. We look at local, regional, and national possibilities for architects. Sometimes the best way forward on a major project is to hire two firms, gaining the strengths of both. Sometimes the way forward is to employ a solid local firm and at the same time to receive the benefit of the wide-ranging, substantial design experience of a nationally respected firm.

Look closely at the firms you are considering as to whether they appear to have the competencies and creativity to achieve the project. We will only get to do this project once. It is critical to select the very best architectural firm.

SELECTION PROCESS

There are three ways of selecting an architect:

1. Architectural study process
2. Architectural interview process
3. Member process

The larger the project, the more likely you are to want to use the architectural study process. Smaller projects will probably work out fine if you use the second or third way.

The architectural interview process does not provide sufficient detail about how the architect would meet your congregation's specific facilities requirements. In this method, several architects are interviewed personally. And they usually share examples of their previous work, but they do not bring a specific proposal for the church with whom they are interviewing. On a smaller, more straightforward project that may be fine.

By member process I mean choosing an architect because she or he is a member of the congregation or is a friend or relative of a member. This method is fraught with pitfalls. You need to select the most competent architect, not the architect who knows everyone or who is known by everyone. Don't count it against an architect if he or she is a member of your congregation, but it's not a point in his or her favor. What counts is not membership or who is friends with whom. What counts is whether the person is the best architect available to do an outstanding job for your congregation and its mission.

Wherever you find an excellent building project done by an architect who was a member of the church, know that it turned out well because the church had a competent architect, not because the architect was a member. Sincerity, membership, and friendship do not necessarily result in an excellent building.

Both the second and third ways have this further dilemma: They both take too long. Without seeing a specific proposal, the church signs a contract and begins meeting with the architect to develop a set of plans. In a good-sized project we will spend nine to twelve months and slowly work our way from plan A to plan B to plan C to plan D. This will have cost us virtually a year.

The architectural study process has several advantages. By following it, you will

- secure the best creativity and thinking of three excellent architectural firms
- have the benefit of their preliminary plan proposals
- have their cost estimates to compare with one another and with your own building project budget
- discover the architect who best suits your mission action plan and who will do the best job for you
- develop a work and fee schedule amenable to you and the architect
- save considerable time (generally six months to a year)
- get to your mission more quickly

The four steps of the architectural study process follow.

1.   Develop a specific list of the essential facilities requirements, improved and/or new, that are central to the mission, and develop the total building project budget.

The building team and task forces develop this list, growing out of your mission action plan, with as much specification as possible. It is not a wish list. It is a streamlined list.

2.   Select three competent architectural firms and invite them to participate in the church's architectural study process.

The building team provides each firm with your long-range mission action plan, the list of essential facilities requirements, and the total building project budget.

3.   The three architectural firms are given a specified period to develop their proposals.

The architectural firms carry their recommendations as far as practical into the schematic design phase to convey their best detailed architectural and planning proposals.

4.   On a given day, each firm presents its detailed proposal to your building committee. Following this, the building team decides which of the three designs most closely serves your mission and which firm you want first to discuss the details of a contract.

With these matters in hand, the building team is in the best position to recommend the architectural firm for the project.

Depending on the extent of the building project, the three architectural firms are given sixty to ninety days to complete their specific proposals. On major projects, the time frame may be somewhat longer. At the same time, many firms have demonstrated their ability to complete their work within ninety days.

During the detailed presentation to the building team, each architectural firm presents these minimum submittals:

Site plan, 1″ = 50′, drawn as a roof-top view, showing the existing and proposed footprint, including ingress and egress, landscape elements, outdoor activity areas, and entrances to all buildings. All parking areas, and the exact number of parking spaces provided, are clearly illustrated.

Floor plans, 1/8″ = 1′, illustrating the organization of the facilities and how this plan fulfills the church's space and budget requirements.

A narrative description, describing the primary design concept, the proposed materials, and construction approach. This account is usually limited to one typewritten page.

Elevations, showing two typical elevations of the proposed space, indicating architectural style, openings, rooflines, materials, and color.

Budget, detailing area tabulations and related budget estimates. These area tabulations should follow the order found in the list of essential facilities requirements.

Each architectural firm is free to present any additional information and drawings it so chooses within the time constraints you've set. Some firms also provide a cross-section drawing, illustrating the vertical and horizontal correlation of all elements and their scale, and an axonometric drawing, showing, as seen from above, the general massing and form of the buildings, their openings, and their relation to exterior areas.

Customarily each firm gives an oral presentation to the building committee along with the submittals. Usually each firm shares its proposal in a fifty-minute session: twenty-five minutes for the presentation and twenty-five minutes for questions from the building team.

Thus, for example, a Saturday schedule might be

9:00–9:50 Firm A

10:00–10:50 Firm B
11:00–11:50 Firm C
12:00–1:30 Building team deliberates over lunch

Ordinarily the team will not decide simply to build design A, B, or C. They will like major features in one, several elements in another, and a couple of suggestions in a third. Actually, over lunch the building team will be quickly on its way to developing design D. With further study and revisions, they will likely build design E or F.

Each architectural firm receives an appropriate fee for their participation in the architectural study process. In return for this fee, the three firms understand that the site plan, floor plans, and so on belong to the church, and the stipend paid confirms that fact. The three firms participate with the hope of concretely demonstrating that they are the best firm for the job.

Contractors invest considerable time and effort in developing a detailed, specific bid. They do so with the hope of receiving the contract. The staff time they invest is the price of doing business. They receive no fee.

The architectural study process is a common practice among businesses, educational institutions, and civic and community groups when they plan building projects. Many competent architects participate in such architectural studies. They are perfectly willing to demonstrate their abilities and creativity to develop an excellent facility.

A few architects may choose not to participate because of prior commitments to other contracts. That is fine, and worth finding out now. Someone who doesn't have the time to participate in an architectural study process probably doesn't have the time to do the project.

Some may be reluctant to participate, feeling they should get a signed contract and begin receiving the full standard fee before they share any of their ideas. But in all sorts of areas people invest considerable time and effort in specific up-front work, with no stipend, before they receive a contract. Interior designers do. Organ builders do. Landscapers do. Contractors do. For every one architect who is reluctant to do so, you'll find five who will.

In selecting three firms to participate in your selection process, you are looking for experience in building facilities in the following arenas:

- schools
- civic and community centers
- recreation centers
- office buildings
- government facilities
- shopping centers
- churches

All seven of these are concerned with space and facilities that serve both large and small groups of people. Some of the best church facilities have been built by architects whose primary experience was in one or more of these arenas. Thus, when selecting three architectural firms, you may want to consult with firms whose best experience has not exclusively been with church facilities.

For example, were we building classrooms and a community life center, we would benefit by inviting two firms whose experience is in educational buildings and recreational facilities, as well as one whose experience is with churches. Thus we would have the best thinking of three outstanding architects.

There are many talented church architects across the country who are well respected because of the high-quality work they've done on a range of church projects. But simply because someone has built a number of churches does not mean that this person is the best match for your project. That architect may have designed one church, and simply done it over again in several different locations. An architect's interest in churches does not automatically result in an excellent building.

The architectural study process is the simplest, best way to ensure that you select the architectural firm and the architect who will build the facilities that suit your specific mission and will bring the building in on time and within budget.

A PRAYER FOR WISDOM

God of mission and of mystery,
    God of majesty and wonder,
        help us to live beyond
            our low self-esteem.
Still our compulsiveness
    toward perfectionism.
        Release our anger.
            Lift our depression.
Grant us wisdom and judgment.
        Give us vision and common sense.
Let our lives be filled with prayer
    and purpose and mission.
        In Jesus' name, amen.

10:

Growing Your Giving

May the God of hope fill you with all joy and
peace in believing, so that by the power of the
Holy Spirit you may abound in hope. *Rom. 15:13*

FUND THE MISSION

Include funding for the mission, not just for construction,
when you raise money to improve present facilities or build
new facilities. There are several reasons for this. First, you
only get a few opportunities to do major, special fund-
raising projects. When you invite people to make three-year
pledges to the building fund, you cannot expect to repeat
that approach to fund-raising again for another three years.

Second, when you include funding for the mission as
well as for the building, you raise more money. A mission-
building fund that has balance, integrity, and broad-based
appeal will inspire people who already give to increase their
contributions generously.

Third, when your building-fund campaign is raising money for both the mission and the building, persons in the congregation who are not now giving will be more likely to give. They can see how their giving will advance two specific, concrete objectives.

Fourth, a mission-building fund campaign will interest people in the community. Given half a chance—that is, given that you let them know what you're doing—some will come forward and give generously to your mission and building. Many people give to mission causes even when they are not members of that group.

Thus, when you put together a building-fund campaign, you can raise money for

- future mission and staffing
- future mission across the planet
- the building
- a beginning endowment for the mission and the building

At the very least, you can develop a building fund campaign that includes two or three of the four.

Future Mission and Staffing

Let's say you have decided to build a community life center to serve your missions with elementary-age children and their families and with youth and their families. Count on having the best community recreation program in the area from the first day on.

You decide, therefore, that you want an excellent community recreation director on staff. The current annual budget cannot fund that staff position. Even if it could, you want the building fund to be a mission-building fund. Thus, in your building-fund campaign you include the funding for the first three years of the position. Following that, the annual budget will pick up the funding.

Or perhaps you decide to build classrooms to serve your mission with preschool children and their families. You count on having the best preschool program in the area from the very first day.

You know, therefore, that you want an excellent preschool director and teachers on your staff. The current annual budget cannot fund that staff position. Even if it could, you want a mission-building fund. You know that much of the funding will come from preschool tuition, and you also know you want to have the best preschool director and staff you can find. Thus, in your building fund you will include some allocation for the first three years to supplement the income from preschool tuition in order to ensure that you can begin strong. Following that, the annual budget and the preschool tuition will pick up whatever funding may be helpful.

Or you decide to construct a new sanctuary to serve your mission with elementary-age children and their families and senior adults and their families. You count on having the best services of worship in the area from day one. You plan to reach and serve many people in the community through worship. And you plan to have more than one service in the new sanctuary.

You know, therefore, that you want excellent music directors on your staff—one for each major worship service. These can each be talented part-time staff. Or, should you already have a full-time music director, that person can build the music groups for one worship service, and new part-time music directors can build the music programs for each of the new services. Consult *Dynamic Worship* for a range of helpful suggestions on how to do this well.

The annual budget will not yet be able to fund this growth in the music staff. Thus, in our building fund you

budget for the first three years of staffing and music program for each worship service. Following that, the annual
budget will pick up the funding.

Future Mission Across the Planet

Some congregations decide to dedicate a certain percentage
of the funds of a building campaign, as they are given, to a
worthwhile mission cause somewhere in the world. Thus,
when people make their building-fund pledge, they have the
confidence that a stated percentage of what they give is going beyond the church to that specific, significant mission
cause. We give to others as well as to ourselves.

Not Just the Building

An excellent mission building team, with a concrete mission
action plan, raises money for the mission, the staffing, and
the building. In our building-fund campaign we plan to
raise a certain amount of money toward improving our present facilities and/or building new facilities. We may also be
drawing on our loan power to assist in that funding.

By contrast, a committee with a meager, unfocused
long-range plan tends to raise money only for the building.
Little time has been spent on the mission plan and much
time on the building plan. They become understandably
anxious about whether they can raise the money needed for
the building. They are anxious because innately they know
people give money to people; uneasy because intuitively
they are aware that they lack specific, compelling people-
pictures to show how the building will be used. They raise
no money at all for the future mission and end up with a
building, but without the mission staffing and mission program to use the building effectively. See *Giving and Stewardship*, particularly the chapter on "Giving Principles," for
further helpful suggestions.

It's like launching a ship without a full crew. The ship just sits in the water, or the limited, underequipped crew struggles to get it under way. The best way forward is to launch an excellent ship with a full crew.

A Beginning Endowment

No annual budget can support the preventative maintenance, ongoing restoration, and major emergency repairs that church buildings need. It is helpful to have an endowment fund specifically for these necessities.

We sometimes raise the seed money for that endowment through the building campaign, knowing that over time people will contribute enduring gifts to the fund and help it grow. Thus, as the building ages, we will in fact have the endowment funds to provide for these items. See *Effective Church Finances*, particularly the chapter on "Enduring Gifts," for further helpful suggestions.

And you are welcome to have a beginning endowment for the mission as well as for the building. We want to give people in both the congregation and the community the opportunity to give enduring gifts to the mission and the building. Thus we would raise the seed money for our endowment to serve the children and youth of the community through the mission program of the community life center.

When you raise the seed money and set a long-term goal, people will give you the enduring gifts to support the mission. When you don't, they simply contribute those enduring gifts somewhere else. People want to give to worthwhile, enduring mission causes.

It's tough to raise money. You'll find it is easier to raise money for mission and building than just for building. The following example is more helpful and easier to do than simply raising money to construct a building alone. You will raise more money from more people, both in the church and in the community.

Future mission and staffing	$100,000
Future mission across the planet	60,000
The new building	900,000
Beginning endowment: mission, building	40,000
	$1,100,000

Or you can do this:

Future mission and staffing	$120,000
Future mission across the planet	80,000
The new building	900,000
	$1,100,000

Or you can do this:

Future mission and staffing	$140,000
The new building	900,000
Beginning endowment: mission, building	60,000
	$1,100,000

Or this:

Future mission and staffing	$200,000
The new building	900,000
	$1,100,000

Any one of these is more helpful and easier to achieve than this:

The new building $900,000

Be at peace about the figures. They will vary widely from one project to the next. The principles hold: People give to people. You will raise more money and help more people with a mission-building campaign that has balance, integrity, and broad appeal, that is mission as well as building.

FUND THE FUTURE

The factors to weigh as you consider your mission and building are

- new persons served
- current persons served
- net new giving
- construction costs, up or down
- interest rates, up or down
- interest on loan

These six factors help you with two important questions: Can we afford to build? Can we afford not to build? Both are equally significant questions. Too many churches ask only the first question. This limits the mission that they in fact can do. Ask both questions—with prayer, compassion, and wisdom.

The sooner we advance our mission, improve our facilities, and build new facilities, the sooner we see these results: new persons served in mission; current persons served more fully; new giving to the mission.

When we delay for one year, we delay the opportunity to serve people for that year. And the net new giving that we

would have received due to increased mission and participation is lost for that year.

Often a year's delay also means that construction costs
and interests rates go up. Thus we both lose the net new giving and end up paying more to build the same building.

Suppose a congregation decides to build a new sanctuary, and preliminary estimates place the construction cost
at $1.5 million. They plan to raise $1.1 million and to borrow $400,000. Their current average worship attendance
is four hundred; their current total giving in a year is
$400,000. They can reasonably see that, by having an excel-
lent first year, their average worship attendance could
increase to six hundred. This would increase the annual giving to $600,000.

Someone in the congregation will be concerned about
keeping down the interest payments on the loan, and they
will suggest delaying construction for a year so as to borrow
less money. Yet when the congregation weighs all six factors
and their relationship to one another, they will most likely
decide to go ahead rather than to delay for a year because of
the advantages in mission growth and giving just described.

Remember that not only is net new giving a function of
net new worship participation, people give to the building
fund when they see progress in the building. Usually the
suggestion to delay the start of construction a year is based
on the premise that people will continue giving regularly toward their three-year building-fund pledge. When there is a
delay, they will still give some; but the pace of the giving is
finally shaped by the pace of mission advancement and
building construction. By delaying, the church would lose
perhaps $150,000 in new giving, which could have been
used to reduce the loan amount. During the year of post-
ponement, by contrast, the church might be lucky to receive
$75,000 to $90,000 in building-fund pledge giving.

Another advantage of not delaying is simple: The congregation builds the building for $1.5 million. Increased construction costs, projected to climb by 11 percent, mean that the building would then cost $1,665,000.

By becoming more quickly a stronger mission congregation, moreover, the church is likelier to pay off the loan sooner. Yes, the church would still borrow the $400,000 and have that extra interest to consider. By delaying, the church would still borrow in the neighborhood of $300,000 if construction costs stayed the same. Yes, it may save by paying interest on $300,000 as opposed to $400,000. But they risk seeing interest rates go up significantly during that year.

The point of the example is to show the importance of thinking through the interrelationship of all six factors involved in advancing your mission and building. Don't get too bogged down in interest rate considerations alone.

POSSIBILITIES FOR GIVING AND FUNDING

God gives you an extraordinary range of possibilities for giving to advance your mission building program. Some are often overlooked. The following brief discussions will help you to consider all possibilities, not just the obvious.

One-time Advance Gifts

Six to nine months before a building campaign, invite the congregation and, as appropriate, the community to give a one-time advance gift as a start-up contribution to help with the initial expenses of launching your program. You may want to bring on board a new staff person to begin developing the mission before the actual construction. You will have initial expenditures of the architectural study process and the preliminary drawings for the building. You can contribute early on to a global mission cause.

Some congregations have a celebration Sunday to raise these one-time advance gifts. Some take a three-week period to give people the opportunity to contribute in advance to the congregation's future. When advance gifts, as a one-time event, are cultivated well at the right time, they increase interest in the later building-fund campaign. People give once, begin to see the results of their gift, and develop long-term ownership of the project.

Major Gifts

The definition of a major gift will vary from one congregation to another. It is important to look for major gifts in the community as well as the congregation. This is particularly valuable when you are launching a significant, worthwhile mission in the community as well as constructing a building.

Three-Year Pledges

To figure what amount of money you can raise over three years, a simple rule of thumb is to take 60 percent of your annual giving and multiply it by three for the three years of the pledge. If, for example, your annual giving is $400,000, you would multiply $240,000 times three and get $720,000. That is the amount of money you can usually raise in the congregation, in addition to major gifts and the other sources of giving we are discussing.

When you have recently had a three-year pledge drive, you might take 50 percent as a base figure, resulting in $600,000 as a reasonable objective. When there is a high density of tithers, or, by contrast, when the church is not delivering well nine of the twelve characteristics of effective congregations, you might consider 40 percent as a base figure, the result being $480,000.

New Giving

The stronger the mission and the more directly it is linked with the congregation, the fuller the increase in particpation—in the mission and the church. The greater the participation, the more net new giving you can reasonably anticipate.

Many congregations don't take into account net new giving. They imagine that the current congregation is going to have to pay for the whole project. This is true only when the project is ingrown and has failed to include a strong community mission focus.

When there is a compelling mission focus, the reasonable result will be an increase in participation and some resultant increase in giving. From one congregation to the next there is a range of variables in projecting net new giving.

The baseline figure for anticipating net new giving is to start with worship attendance. Given our mission building project, were there to be an increase of 40 percent in average worship attendance, giving would eventually increase by 40 percent. Let's say the current worship attendance is four hundred and the current giving is $400,000. With a 40 percent increase in average worship attendance, the net new giving will eventually be an additional $160,000. This won't happen overnight—it will lag by three to five months, but it will be there.

Decide the new giving resources you want to have available for the congregation's mission as you look to the coming fifty years. Take into account

- the more persons served in mission, the more persons who are likely to participate in the mission;

- the stronger the worship attendance, the more giving that will be available for mission;

- the more constructive your investment in mission, staffing, and programming, the likelier it is that giving will grow;
- the net new giving during the years to come in relation to the investment in the facilities.

The correlation is between persons served in mission, worship attendance, and giving. The correlation is not between membership and giving. A congregation whose average worship attendance is eight hundred and whose giving is $800,000 will see its giving grow to $1.2 million when its worship attendance is twelve hundred. Over a twenty-year period this is a considerable amount of new giving that will advance God's mission.

The money is for the mission. Just because more worship services or a larger sanctuary will generate more giving, we have no excuse for extravagance—we must take seriously the up-front costs of the facilities. Nor do we have an excuse to overbuild. It is important to build a suitable match to the mission.

Weighing the initial investment in relation to the long-term giving for the mission invites your best wisdom. Not overbuilding or underbuilding also invites your best wisdom.

Local Community Gifts

When we have a compelling mission in the community, some people in the community (who are not members of the church) will give you money to help with the mission.

One of the most respected and trusted mission groups on the planet—whose compelling mission is with the poor—receives most of its funding from persons who are not members of the group. The two primary reasons more congregations do not receive community gifts are (1) they don't have a compelling mission in the community, and (2) they don't think to ask.

As you develop your campaign, form a task force of people who know how to ask for community gifts and who have a sense for what groupings, persons, and businesses in the community would be interested in contributing their support. People in the community will give generously because of the integrity of the mission you are developing.

Friends of the Church Who Live Elsewhere

There are many former members or participants who think well of your church. They would be glad to help with a one-time contribution. There are family members of people in your congregation who would be interested in helping with a one-time gift to the mission.

Memorial Gifts

Consider inviting people to give memorial gifts to support the mission you are advancing as well as the building you are constructing. Many people will glad for the opportunity to contribute a gift that honors the memory of a friend or loved one and that will advance the mission.

Endowment Gifts

There may be some endowment gifts given during the building-fund campaign. Frequently we include in the campaign design an amount for seed money to endow the mission and building. Other endowment gifts will be pledged now and will come to the church later. These endowment gifts are invested and act as the principal; the earned interest is for use in the mission or building, as designated by the donor.

Short-term, Special Fund-Raising Projects

Many congregations raise a portion of their funding for a mission building project through specific projects. These projects may be organized by an adult church school class, your women's or men's group, a youth group, the choir, and so forth.

Many such projects make it possible for the larger community, as well as the congregation, to offer their support. This grows both the giving and the community's awareness and ownership of your mission.

Saleable Church Assets

Has your church been given a piece of property elsewhere that it does not plan to use? Now may be the time to sell it and use the proceeds to support the mission.

The same is true of a wide range of assets the church may have been given. Think through what property, equipment, stocks, bonds, and the like may be helpful to your project and whether now is the appropriate time to sell them. Be sure to respect any restrictions the donor may have placed on the gift.

Special Grants

Depending on the nature of your mission, you may discover that securing a grant is possible. For example, one congregation decided to have a mission with elementary-age children through an excellent after-school program. A private foundation contributed a grant of $250,000 to assist the project.

While it is sometimes difficult to work through the grant application process, congregations with a compelling mission in the community are in a strong position to consider this possibility.

Denominational Support

This may be a source of some funding, although in recent years the ability of some denominations to help has been limited. Certainly it is an avenue worth exploring.

Other Possibilities

An excellent idea may occur to you that doesn't quite fit into one of the categories just discussed. Include it here.

Loan Power

One thing any congregation has is a certain amount of loan power. I developed this term to indicate that whatever loan capacity your congregation has can be an important means for advancing your mission. This loan power is to be used wisely and well.

There are a number of variables to consider in assessing the loan power available to a given congregation. Among these variables, three are helpful to study: the current building campaign pledges, the immediate and long-term projected net new giving, and any follow-on building campaign. These three, plus any later major gifts and grants, will help you service whatever loan power you decide to exercise. To service a loan means to have giving adequate to meet the payments for a certain time period. The payments may be monthly, quarterly, yearly, or on whatever schedule is mutually agreeable with the lender.

When you have considered these possibilities, think through the strength of your congregation. As a general rule (and there are exceptions), a healthy congregation can usually take out a loan equal to two times its current total giving. A congregation with total giving of $400,000, for instance, has a loan power of $800,000. That does not mean that this congregation should rush out and borrow that amount of money.

It does mean that this congregation can do two things: First, it can explore all the possibilities of giving available to it. These should be investigated before the church taps into its loan power.

The more people who give to your mission-building objectives, the more people who feel ownership of them. When you go too quickly to the bank to exercise your loan power, you lose both the money people will give and their long-term ownership of the mission. And when we move too quickly to exercise our loan power, we end up borrowing more money than we need to.

Second, a congregation can exercise its reasonable loan power to underwrite the mission. Some people say they don't want to borrow—ever. Yet many people have a loan on their home, on their car, and so forth. What gets some people into trouble is overborrowing. Other people underborrow or never borrow.

With churches it works both ways as well. Some churches get into trouble because they overbuild and thus overborrow and thereby overburden themselves with too much debt. They become preoccupied with the monthly payments on the loan. They become too concerned with debt retirement.

Too many other churches, particularly strong, growing congregations, get into trouble because they underborrow at precisely the moment when they can best advance their mission. They lose their momentum. They become money conscious rather than mission conscious.

It takes wisdom and prayer to puzzle through what range of loan power makes sense for a congregation to exercise. Generally speaking, congregations have a loan power in the ranges shown in Table 10.1.

Table 10.1

Strength of Congregation	Loan Power in Relation to Annual Giving
strong, healthy, rapidly growing	2–4 times plus
strong, healthy, growing	
stable	1–2 times
weak, declining	1/2–1 time
dying	

I encourage congregations to use their loan power wisely and well. Don't overborrow or underborrow. Consider all the possibilities for giving. Consider the compelling nature of your mission. Consider your mission action plan. Consider the present and emerging strengths of your congregation. Then put together the best possible combination of giving resources and loan power that will advance your mission.

For your mission-building campaign, take into account all of the giving possibilities available to you. Table 10.2 will help you discover all of your financial resources and realistically assess your funding potential.

Factor the total giving possibilities, keeping in mind that some of them will be used to pay back any loan power you decide to exercise. Having done that, you will have a reasonable idea of the total financial resources available for your mission building project.

Table 10.2 Giving and Funding Analysis

	Low	Estimates Medium	High	Realistic
Possibilities				
one-time advance gifts				
major gifts				
three-year pledges				
new giving				
local community gifts				
friends of the church				
memorial gifts				
endowment gifts				
short-term projects				
saleable church assets				
foundation grants				
denominational support				
other possibilities				
loan power				

With God's help, you will find the funds for your mission. With God's help, you will choose wisely to fund your future. With God's help, you can grow your possibilities for giving and exercise your loan power—all for the purpose of advancing the specific mission to which God is inviting you.

A PRAYER FOR GIVING

Living God,
>   help us to grow a life of mission and giving.
>>   May we think and act as part of a winning cause.

May we discover more fully the gift of generosity
>   with which you have blessed us.

Grant that we will live forward to our best possibilities.
>   Give us ears, eyes, and heart
>>   to discover your calling in our lives.

>   May we give generously and graciously to people.

Help us to relax, have fun, enjoy life, to live in Christ.

>>   Give us mission, grace, and peace. Amen.

11 :

Mission and Hope

In him was life, and the life was the light of men.
The light shines in the darkness, and the darkness
has not overcome it. *John 1:4–5*

THE HOLY GIFTS OF LIFE AND MISSION

Live the mission, and you will find life in it. In Christ is life,
and the life is the light of humankind. In Christ is mission;
the light of mission shines in the darkness, and the darkness
cannot overcome it.

Life is the gift of God. It is not merely an idle pastime,
to be wasted in flurry, fluff, and fury. Life is to be shared
richly in the name of Christ.

There is a sacramental quality to life. God is fully present everywhere; all of creation is a sign of God's grace. The
gift of life to each of us is a sign of God's generosity. It is a
holy gift, to be treasured and lived well, with wonder and
awe at its mystery.

Mission too is the gift of God. We share mission because God shares mission with us. In mission we discover
that our lives are worthwhile. We have focus and are centered. We know what is truly important in life.

There is a sacramental spirit to mission and wonder and mystery in mission. In the act of mission the precious, sacred nature of all life is confirmed. Mission is a sign of God's grace, to be treasured and shared well. In the act of mission, God is fully present. In the moment of mission we know our lives count.

PURPOSE

In mission we find purpose.

People seek, earnestly, desperately, some purpose and meaning for their life. Older understandings of agrarian and industrial cultures have served their age and time. Ours is an emerging new civilization.

The knowledge explosion, the technological explosion, the galaxies—these are our companions.

We live in a time of megadigm shift. A megadigm is a collection of paradigms interacting with one another and thereby creating, not a singular new world view, but a new, multi-dimensional world view. This is a time of multiple paradigm shifts happening simultaneously, interacting rapidly with one another. Our time is more dynamic and complex than simply a paradigm shift from one way of thinking to another.

It is not so much that we need a solution. What we need is a direction. We are at the beginning of an age. We need a way forward as we help people make sense of life, for this time, in the light of the gospel.

God invites us to run and not be weary. It is not an invitation to wait and study, meet and discuss. We are invited to run, with compassion, looking to Christ for direction.

With creativity and imagination, help people discover a sense of direction for their life in mission. With compassion and courage, help them grow in mission. Share joy and hope in the name of Christ. Share simplicity amid ambiguity, clarity amid chaos.

As we share mission we participate in a new openness to the leadings of God. We discover purpose, value, and meaning in life. We are baptized anew into new life in Christ.

We share in the new covenant, which invites us to live beyond older ways and older understandings to a new relationship with God and with one another. We share in the sacrament of sacrifice and compassion, of community and covenant.

We participate in the sacrament of new hope, future, resurrection. The former things have passed away, and the new has come. In the act of mission the sacrament of service happens.

God invites us to mission. God invites our lives to count in new ways.

THE SOURCE OF OUR POWER

Praise God for the mission and that our lives have purpose. The power comes through helping people with their hurts and hopes in the name of Christ. Power is not in the things of this world, as enticing and beguiling as they seem. Power is not in the perks, the prestige, and the promotions the world confers. Power is not in the fleeting flimsies that come and go, wither and fade.

Now, people do increasingly feel that the decisions that shape their lives and destinies are made somewhere else by someone else. A sense of powerlessness has spread across the land. Enduring power is found in mission.

With humility and compassion, we give ourselves to serve the community, the world that God gives us to serve. We pray that we will share well the strengths with which God blesses us. We consecrate the mission to which God invites us and the mortar that serves the mission.

God invites us to mission with compassion, to vision with common sense, to strong hopes with solid priorities. We are invited to mission without wishful thinking and to vision without grandiosity. We are invited to share our best creativity and encouragement. We are invited to build well—with simplicity, wisdom, and compelling compassion.

We will leave room for the future and remain open to the mission that may unfold in the years to come. We don't need to decide now what all of those future missions might be. We do have some hopes and hunches. Our long-range plan will live out these hopes. And we will remain open to the possibilities God puts before us.

Enduring power is found in giving, not grasping, in sharing, not striving, in serving, not preserving. We are invited to put on

> compassion, kindness, lowliness, meekness, and patience, . . . forgiving each other. . . . And above all these put on love, which binds everything together in perfect harmony. And let the peace of Christ rule in your hearts, to which indeed you were called in the one body. And be thankful. *Col. 3:12–15*

When we lose ourselves in mission, we find ourselves anew, renewed. When we give ourselves away, we find God every day. Power is in serving, not controlling. It is power, not as the world understands it, but in the way God bestows it.

HOPE

The future is God's gift to us. The future stirs our deepest creativity and calls for our best ingenuity, imagination, and originality. The future is God's way of leading us forward.

As we share mission we discover life anew. The act of mission teaches us new lessons and helps us discover new ways in Christ. It is precisely in mission, with its joys and difficulties, its press and problems, that we discover growth—not in size or numbers but in new insights, new compassion, new strengths. We find a deeper humility and a more profound sense of service. In mission we become new creatures in Christ.

As we grow and learn, we find that new forms of mission emerge and new ways to serve are revealed. Certainty and continuity are, paradoxically, found in opening ourselves to newness, with the help of God.

We discover hope, which is a gift to us from our mission. Hope is in the cause, not the career. If we become preoccupied with our career, God will step in to help us discover the mission in fresh ways.

> We rejoice in our hope of sharing the glory of God. More than that we rejoice in our sufferings, knowing that suffering produces endurance, and endurance produces character, and character produces hope, and hope does not disappoint us, because God's love has been poured into our hearts through the Holy Spirit which has been given to us. *Rom. 5:2–5*

Our God goes us before us, leading us to the future that God promises and is preparing. It is not that the future breaks in upon us; the future invites, leads, draws us to renewed life.

Our hope is in the resurrection. In the sacrament of mission, the resurrection happens. Life, purpose, power, hope—these are the gifts and the strengths that God gives us for mission.

The mission prevails over change, conflict, discontinuity, defeat. The mission of God is eternal, and because of that we are steady, confident, and joyful as we live out the mission.

Christ comes to us and shows us the power of sacrifice and love, thereby giving us a vision of what is genuinely worthwhile in life. The Spirit too sustains us. We sense the moving, stirring, living presence of the Spirit in our lives.

We pray that many people discover the spirit of compassion, the sense of community, the strength of hope in mission. May God's blessings of life, purpose, power, and hope be present with us. May our lives count well for God's mission.

God has blessed us. Be in prayer. Build well for effective mission. The light shines.

A CONGREGATIONAL RESPONSE
FOR THE RESURRECTION

Grace is stronger than law.

> *We are the People of Grace.*

Compassion is stronger than legalism.

> *We are the People of Compassion.*

Easter is stronger than Good Friday.

> *We are the Easter People.*

The open tomb is stronger than the bloodied cross.

> *We are the People of the Open Tomb.*

The Risen Lord is stronger than the dead Jesus.

> *We are the People of the Risen Lord.*
> *We are the Resurrection People.*
> *We are the People of Hope.*

Index